PENGUIN BOOKS

A NEW EARTH

DISCARD

Eckhart Tolle was born in Germany. When he was twenty-nine, a profound spiritual transformation virtually dissolved his old identity and radically changed the course of his life. He is now a counsellor and spiritual teacher, and the author of *The Power of Now*, *Practising the Power of Now* and *Stillness Speaks*. He lives in Vancouver.

ALSO BY ECKHART TOLLE

*The Power of Now*

*Practicing the Power of Now*

*Stillness Speaks*

# A NEW EARTH

*Awakening to Your Life's Purpose*

ECKHART TOLLE

PENGUIN BOOKS

PENGUIN BOOKS

Published by the Penguin Group
Penguin Books Ltd, 80 Strand, London WC2R ORL, England
Penguin Group (USA) Inc., 375 Hudson Street, New York, New York 10014, USA
Penguin Group (Canada), 90 Eglinton Avenue East, Suite 700, Toronto, Ontario, Canada M4P 2Y3
(a division of Pearson Penguin Canada Inc.)
Penguin Ireland, 25 St Stephen's Green, Dublin 2, Ireland (a division of Penguin Books Ltd)
Penguin Group (Australia), 250 Camberwell Road,
Camberwell, Victoria 3124, Australia (a division of Pearson Australia Group Pty Ltd)
Penguin Books India Pvt Ltd, 11 Community Centre,
Panchsheel Park, New Delhi – 110 017, India
Penguin Group (NZ), cnr Airborne and Rosedale Roads, Albany,
Auckland 1310, New Zealand (a division of Pearson New Zealand Ltd)
Penguin Books (South Africa) (Pty) Ltd, 24 Sturdee Avenue,
Rosebank, Johannesburg 2196, South Africa

Penguin Books Ltd, Registered Offices: 80 Strand, London WC2R ORL, England

www.penguin.com

First published in the USA by Dutton, a member of Penguin Group (USA) Inc. 2005
First published in Great Britain by Michael Joseph 2005
Published in Penguin Books 2006

6

Copyright © Eckhart Tolle, 2005
All rights reserved

The moral right of the author has been asserted

Printed in England by Clays Ltd, St Ives plc

ISBN-13: 978-0-141-02759-3

# CONTENTS

CHAPTER THREE

*The Core of Ego* · 59

CHAPTER FOUR

*Role-playing: The Many Faces of the Ego* · 85

CHAPTER FIVE

*The Pain-Body* · 129

CHAPTER SIX

## Breaking Free · 161

CHAPTER SEVEN

## Finding Who You Truly Are · 185

CHAPTER EIGHT

## The Discovery of Inner Space · 223

CHAPTER NINE

## Your Inner Purpose · 257

CHAPTER TEN

## A New Earth · 279

# A NEW EARTH

## CHAPTER ONE

# The Flowering of Human Consciousness

## EVOCATION

Earth, 114 million years ago, one morning just after sunrise: The first flower ever to appear on the planet opens up to receive the rays of the sun. Prior to this momentous event that heralds an evolutionary transformation in the life of plants, the planet had already been covered in vegetation for millions of years. The first flower probably did not survive for long, and flowers must have remained rare and isolated phenomena, since conditions were most likely not yet favorable for a widespread flowering to occur. One day, however, a critical threshold was reached, and suddenly there would have been an explosion of color and scent all over the planet—if a perceiving consciousness had been there to witness it.

I

Much later, those delicate and fragrant beings we call flowers would come to play an essential part in the evolution of consciousness of another species. Humans would increasingly be drawn to and fascinated by them. As the consciousness of human beings developed, flowers were most likely the first thing they came to value that had no utilitarian purpose for them, that is to say, was not linked in some way to survival. They provided inspiration to countless artists, poets, and mystics. Jesus tells us to contemplate the flowers and learn from them how to live. The Buddha is said to have given a "silent sermon" once during which he held up a flower and gazed at it. After a while, one of those present, a monk called Mahakasyapa, began to smile. He is said to have been the only one who had understood the sermon. According to legend, that smile (that is to say, realization) was handed down by twenty-eight successive masters and much later became the origin of Zen.

Seeing beauty in a flower could awaken humans, however briefly, to the beauty that is an essential part of their own innermost being, their true nature. The first recognition of beauty was one of the most significant events in the evolution of human consciousness. The feelings of joy and love are intrinsically connected to that recognition. Without our fully realizing it, flowers would become for us an expression in form of that which is most high, most sacred, and ultimately formless within ourselves. Flowers, more fleeting, more ethereal, and more delicate than the plants out of which they emerged, would become like messengers from another realm, like a bridge between the world of physical forms and the formless. They not only had a scent that was delicate and pleasing to humans, but also brought a fragrance from the realm of spirit. Using the word "enlightenment" in a wider sense than the conventionally accepted one, we could look upon flowers as the enlightenment of plants.

Any life-form in any realm—mineral, vegetable, animal, or human—can be said to undergo "enlightenment." It is, however, an extremely rare occurrence since it is more than an evolutionary progression: It also implies a discontinuity in its development, a leap to an entirely different level of Being and, most important, a lessening of materiality.

What could be heavier and more impenetrable than a rock, the densest of all forms? And yet some rocks undergo a change in their molecular structure, turn into crystals, and so become transparent to the light. Some carbons, under inconceivable heat and pressure, turn into diamonds, and some heavy minerals into other precious stones.

Most crawling reptilians, the most earthbound of all creatures, have remained unchanged for millions of years. Some, however, grew feathers and wings and turned into birds, thus defying the force of gravity that had held them for so long. They didn't become better at crawling or walking, but transcended crawling and walking entirely.

Since time immemorial, flowers, crystals, precious stones,

and birds have held special significance for the human spirit. Like all life-forms, they are, of course, temporary manifestations of the underlying one Life, one Consciousness. Their special significance and the reason why humans feel such fascination for and affinity with them can be attributed to their ethereal quality.

Once there is a certain degree of Presence, of still and alert attention in human beings' perceptions, they can sense the divine life essence, the one indwelling consciousness or spirit in every creature, every life-form, recognize it as one with their own essence and so love it as themselves. Until this happens, however, most humans see only the outer forms, unaware of the inner essence, just as they are unaware of their own essence and identify only with their own physical and psychological form.

In the case of a flower, a crystal, precious stone, or bird, however, even someone with little or no Presence can occasionally sense that there is more there than the mere physical existence of that form, without knowing that this is the reason why he or she is drawn toward it, feels an affinity with it. Because of its ethereal nature, its form obscures the indwelling spirit to a lesser degree than is the case with other life-forms. The exception to this are all newborn life-forms—babies, puppies, kittens, lambs, and so on. They are fragile, delicate, not yet firmly established in materiality. An innocence, a sweetness and beauty that are not of this world still shine through them. They delight even relatively insensitive humans.

So when you are alert and contemplate a flower, crystal, or bird without naming it mentally, it becomes a window for you into the formless. There is an inner opening, however slight, into the realm of spirit. This is why these three "en-lightened" life-forms have played such an important part in the evolution of human consciousness since ancient times; why, for example, the jewel in the lotus flower is a central symbol of Buddhism and a white bird, the dove, signifies the Holy Spirit in Christianity. They have been preparing the ground for a more profound shift in planetary consciousness that is destined to take place in the human species. This is the spiritual awakening that we are beginning to witness now.

## THE PURPOSE OF THIS BOOK

Is humanity ready for a transformation of consciousness, an inner flowering so radical and profound that compared to it the flowering of plants, no matter how beautiful, is only a pale reflection? Can human beings lose the density of their conditioned mind structures and become like crystals or precious stones, so to speak, transparent to the light of consciousness? Can they defy the gravitational pull of materialism and materiality and rise above identification with form that keeps the ego in place and condemns them to imprisonment within their own personality?

The possibility of such a transformation has been the central message of the great wisdom teachings of humankind. The messengers—Buddha, Jesus, and others, not all of them known—were humanity's early flowers. They were precursors, rare and precious beings. A widespread flowering was not yet possible at that time, and their message became largely misunderstood and often greatly distorted. It certainly did not transform human behavior, except in a small minority of people.

Is humanity more ready now than at the time of those early teachers? Why should this be so? What can you do, if anything, to bring about or accelerate this inner shift? What is it that characterizes the old egoic state of consciousness, and by what signs is the new emerging consciousness recognized? These and other essential questions will be addressed in this book. More important, this book itself is a transformational device that has come out of the arising new consciousness. The ideas and concepts presented here may be important, but they are secondary. They are no more than signposts pointing toward awakening. As you read, a shift takes place within you.

This book's main purpose is not to add new information or beliefs to your mind or to try to convince you of anything, but to bring about a shift in consciousness, that is to say, to awaken. In that sense, this book is not "interesting." Interesting means you can keep your distance, play around with ideas and concepts in your mind, agree or disagree. This book is about you. It will change your state of consciousness or it will be meaningless. It can only awaken those who are ready. Not everyone is ready yet, but many are, and with each person who awakens, the momentum in the collective consciousness grows, and it becomes easier for others. If you don't know what awakening means, read on. Only by awakening can you know the true meaning of that word. A glimpse is enough to initiate the awakening process, which is irreversible. For some, that glimpse will come while reading this book. For many others who may not even have realized it, the process has already begun. This book will help them recognize it. For some, it may have begun through loss or suffering; for others, through coming into contact with a spiritual teacher or teaching, through reading *The Power of Now* or some other spiritually alive and therefore transformational book—or any combination of the above. If the awakening process has begun in you, the reading of this book will accelerate and intensify it.

An essential part of the awakening is the recognition of the unawakened you, the ego as it thinks, speaks, and acts, as well as the recognition of the collectively conditioned mental processes that perpetuate the unawakened state.

That is why this book shows the main aspects of the ego and how they operate in the individual as well as in the collective. This is important for two related reasons: The first is that unless you know the basic mechanics behind the workings of the ego, you won't recognize it, and it will trick you into identifying with it again and again. This means it takes you over, an imposter pretending to be you. The second reason is that the act of recognition itself is one of the ways in which awakening happens. When you recognize the unconsciousness in you, that which makes the recognition possible *is* the arising consciousness, *is* awakening. You cannot fight against the ego and win, just as you cannot fight against darkness. The light of consciousness is all that is necessary. You are that light.

## OUR INHERITED DYSFUNCTION

If we look more deeply into humanity's ancient religions and spiritual traditions, we will find that underneath the many surface differences there are two core insights that most of them agree on. The words they use to describe those insights differ, yet they all point to a twofold fundamental truth. The first part of this truth is the realization that the "normal" state of mind of most human beings contains a strong element of what we might call dysfunction or even madness. Certain teachings at the heart of Hinduism perhaps come closest to seeing this dysfunction as a form of collective mental illness. They call it *maya,* the veil of delusion. Ramana Maharshi, one of the greatest Indian sages, bluntly states: "The mind is maya."

Buddhism uses different terms. According to the Buddha, the human mind in its normal state generates *dukkha,* which can be translated as suffering, unsatisfactoriness, or just plain misery. He sees it as a characteristic of the human condition. Wherever you go, whatever you do, says the Buddha, you will encounter *dukkha,* and it will manifest in every situation sooner or later.

According to Christian teachings, the normal collective state of humanity is one of "original sin." *Sin* is a word that has been greatly misunderstood and misinterpreted. Literally translated from the ancient Greek in which the New Testament was written, to sin means to miss the mark, as an archer who misses the target, so to sin means to *miss the point* of human existence. It means to live unskillfully, blindly, and thus to suffer and cause suffering. Again, the term, stripped of its cultural baggage and misinterpretations, points to the dysfunction inherent in the human condition.

The achievements of humanity are impressive and undeniable. We have created sublime works of music, literature, painting, architecture, and sculpture. More recently, science and technology have brought about radical changes in the way we live and have enabled us to do and create things that would have been considered miraculous even two hundred years ago. No doubt: The human mind is highly intelligent. Yet its very intelligence is tainted by madness. Science and technology have magnified the destructive impact that the dysfunction of the human mind has upon the planet, other life-forms, and upon humans themselves. That is why the history of the twentieth century is where that dysfunction, that collective insanity, can be most clearly recognized. A further factor is that this dysfunction is actually intensifying and accelerating.

The First World War broke out in 1914. Destructive and cruel wars, motivated by fear, greed, and the desire for power, had been common occurrences throughout human history, as had slavery, torture, and widespread violence inflicted for religious and ideological reasons. Humans suffered more at the hands of each other than through natural disasters. By the year 1914, however, the highly intelligent human mind had invented not only the internal combustion engine, but also bombs, machine guns, submarines, flame throwers, and poison gas. Intelligence in the service of madness! In static trench warfare in France and Belgium, millions of men perished to gain a few miles of mud. When the war was over in 1918, the survivors looked in horror and incomprehension upon the devastation left behind: ten million human beings killed and many more maimed or disfigured. Never before had human madness been so destructive in its effect, so clearly visible. Little did they know that this was only the beginning.

By the end of the century, the number of people who

died a violent death at the hand of their fellow humans would rise to more than one hundred million. They died not only through wars between nations, but also through mass exterminations and genocide, such as the murder of twenty million "class enemies, spies, and traitors" in the Soviet Union under Stalin or the unspeakable horrors of the Holocaust in Nazi Germany. They also died in countless smaller internal conflicts, such as the Spanish civil war or during the Khmer Rouge regime in Cambodia when a quarter of that country's population was murdered.

We only need to watch the daily news on television to realize that the madness has not abated, that it is continuing into the twenty-first century. Another aspect of the collective dysfunction of the human mind is the unprecedented violence that humans are inflicting on other life-forms and the planet itself—the destruction of oxygen-producing forests and other plant and animal life; ill-treatment of animals in factory farms; and poisoning of rivers, oceans, and air. Driven by greed, ignorant of their connectedness to the whole, humans persist in behavior that, if continued unchecked, can only result in their own destruction.

The collective manifestations of the insanity that lies at the heart of the human condition constitute the greater part of human history. It is to a large extent a history of madness. If the history of humanity were the clinical case history of a single human being, the diagnosis would have to be: chronic paranoid delusions, a pathological propensity to commit murder and acts of extreme violence and cruelty against his perceived "enemies"—his own unconsciousness projected outward. Criminally insane, with a few brief lucid intervals.

Fear, greed, and the desire for power are the psychological motivating forces not only behind warfare and violence between nations, tribes, religions, and ideologies, but also the cause of incessant conflict in personal relationships. They bring about a distortion in your perception of other people and yourself. Through them, you misinterpret every situation, leading to misguided action designed to rid you of fear and satisfy your need for *more*, a bottomless hole that can never be filled.

It is important to realize, however, that fear, greed, and the desire for power are not the dysfunction that we are speaking of, but are themselves created by the dysfunction, which is a deep-seated collective delusion that lies within the mind of each human being. A number of spiritual teachings tell us to let go of fear and desire. But those spiritual practices are usually unsuccessful. They haven't gone to the root of the dysfunction. Fear, greed, and desire for power are not the ultimate causal factors. Trying to become a good or better human being sounds like a commendable and high-minded thing to do, yet it is an endeavor you cannot ultimately succeed in unless there is a shift in consciousness. This is because it is still part of the same dysfunction, a more subtle and rarified form of self-enhancement, of desire for more and a strengthening of one's conceptual identity, one's self-image. You do not become good by trying to be good, but by finding the goodness that is already within you, and allowing that goodness to emerge. But it can only emerge if something fundamental changes in your state of consciousness.

The history of Communism, originally inspired by noble ideals, clearly illustrates what happens when people attempt to change external reality—create a new earth—without any prior change in their inner reality, their state of consciousness. They make plans without taking into account the blueprint for dysfunction that every human being carries within: the ego.

## THE ARISING NEW CONSCIOUSNESS

Most ancient religions and spiritual traditions share the common insight—that our "normal" state of mind is marred by a fundamental defect. However, out of this insight into the nature of the human condition—we may call it the bad news—arises a second insight: the good news of the possibility of a radical transformation of human consciousness. In Hindu teachings (and sometimes in Buddhism also), this transformation is called *enlightenment*. In the teachings of Jesus, it is *salvation*, and in Buddhism, it is *the end of suffering*. *Liberation* and *awakening* are other terms used to describe this transformation.

The greatest achievement of humanity is not its works of art, science, or technology, but the recognition of its own dysfunction, its own madness. In the distant past, this recognition already came to a few individuals. A man called Gautama Siddhartha, who lived 2,600 years ago in India, was perhaps the first who saw it with absolute clarity. Later, the title Buddha was conferred upon him. *Buddha* means "the awakened one." At about the same time, another of humanity's early awakened teachers emerged in China. His name was Lao Tzu. He left a record of his teaching in the form of one of the most profound spiritual books ever written, the *Tao Te Ching*.

To recognize one's own insanity is, of course, the arising of sanity, the beginning of healing and transcendence. A new dimension of consciousness had begun to emerge on the planet, a first tentative flowering. Those rare individuals then spoke to their contemporaries. They spoke of sin, of suffering, of delusion. They said, "Look how you live. See what you are doing, the suffering you create." They then pointed to the possibility of awakening from the collective nightmare of "normal" human existence. They showed the way.

The world was not yet ready for them, and yet they were a vital and necessary part of human awakening. Inevitably, they were mostly misunderstood by their contemporaries, as well as by subsequent generations. Their teachings, although both simple and powerful, became distorted and misinterpreted, in some cases even as they were recorded in writing by their disciples. Over the centuries, many things were added that had nothing to do with the original teachings, but were reflections of a fundamental misunderstanding. Some of the teachers were ridiculed, reviled, or killed; others came to be worshiped as gods. Teachings that pointed the way beyond the dysfunction of the human mind, the way out of the collective insanity, were distorted and became themselves part of the insanity.

And so religions, to a large extent, became divisive rather than unifying forces. Instead of bringing about an ending of violence and hatred through a realization of the fundamental oneness of all life, they brought more violence and hatred, more divisions between people as well as between different religions and even within the same religion. They became ideologies, belief systems people could identify with and so use them to enhance their false sense of self. Through them, they could make themselves "right" and others "wrong" and thus define their identity through their enemies, the "others," the "nonbelievers" or "wrong believers" who not infrequently they saw themselves justified in killing. Man made "God" in his own image. The eternal, the infinite, and unnameable was reduced to a mental idol that you had to believe in and worship as "my god" or "our god."

And yet . . . and yet . . . in spite of all the insane deeds perpetrated in the name of religion, the Truth to which they point still shines at their core. It still shines, however dimly, through layers upon layers of distortion and misinterpretation. It is unlikely, however, that you will be able to perceive it there unless you have at least already had glimpses of that Truth within yourself. Throughout history, there have always been rare individuals who experienced a shift in consciousness and so realized within themselves that toward which all religions point. To describe that nonconceptual Truth, they then used the conceptual framework of their own religions.

Through some of those men and women, "schools" or movements developed within all major religions that represented not only a rediscovery, but in some cases an intensification of the light of the original teaching. This is how Gnosticism and mysticism came into existence in early and medieval Christianity, Sufism in the Islamic religion, Hasidism and Kabbala in Judaism, Advaita Vedanta in Hinduism, Zen and Dzogchen in Buddhism. Most of these schools were iconoclastic. They did away with layers upon layers of deadening conceptualization and mental belief structures, and for this reason most of them were viewed with suspicion and often hostility by the established religious hierarchies. Unlike mainstream religion, their teachings emphasized realization and inner transformation. It is through those esoteric schools or movements that the major religions regained the transformative power of the original teachings, although in most cases, only a small minority of people had access to them. Their numbers were never large enough to have any significant impact on the deep collective unconsciousness of the majority. Over time, some of those schools themselves became too rigidly formalized or conceptualized to remain effective.

## SPIRITUALITY AND RELIGION

What is the role of the established religions in the arising of the new consciousness? Many people are already aware of the difference between spirituality and religion. They realize that having a belief system—a set of thoughts that you regard as the absolute truth—does not make you spiritual no matter what the nature of those beliefs is. In fact, the more you make your thoughts (beliefs) into your identity, the more cut off you are from the spiritual dimension within yourself. Many "religious" people are stuck at that level. They equate truth with thought, and as they are completely identified with thought (their mind), they claim to be in sole possession of the truth in an unconscious attempt to protect their identity. They don't realize the limitations of thought. Unless you believe (think) exactly as they do, you are wrong in their eyes, and in the not-too-distant past, they would have felt justified in killing you for that. And some still do, even now.

The new spirituality, the transformation of consciousness, is arising to a large extent outside of the structures of the existing institutionalized religions. There were always pockets of spirituality even in mind-dominated religions, although the institutionalized hierarchies felt threatened by them and often tried to suppress them. A large-scale opening of spirituality outside of the religious structures is an entirely new development. In the past, this would have been inconceivable, especially in the West, the most mind-dominated of all cultures, where the Christian church had a virtual franchise on spirituality. You couldn't just stand up and give a spiritual talk or publish a spiritual book unless you were sanctioned by the church, and if you were not, they would quickly silence you. But now, even within certain churches and religions, there are signs of change. It is heartwarming, and one is grateful for even the slightest signs of openness, such as Pope John Paul II visiting a mosque as well as a synagogue.

Partly as a result of the spiritual teachings that have arisen outside the established religions, but also due to an influx of the ancient Eastern wisdom teachings, a growing number of followers of traditional religions are able to let go of identification with form, dogma, and rigid belief systems and discover the original depth that is hidden within their own spiritual tradition at the same time as they discover the depth within themselves. They realize that how "spiritual" you are has nothing to do with what you believe but everything to do with your state of consciousness. This, in turn, determines how you act in the world and interact with others.

Those unable to look beyond form become even more deeply entrenched in their beliefs, that is to say, in their mind. We are witnessing not only an unprecedented influx of consciousness at this time but also an entrenchment and intensification of the ego. Some religious institutions will be open to the new consciousness; others will harden their doctrinal positions and become part of all those other man-made structures through which the collective ego will defend itself and "fight back." Some churches, sects, cults, or religious movements are basically collective egoic entities, as rigidly identified with their mental positions as the followers of any political ideology that is closed to any alternative interpretation of reality.

But the ego is destined to dissolve, and all its ossified structures, whether they be religious or other institutions, corporations, or governments, will disintegrate from within, no matter how deeply entrenched they appear to be. The most rigid structures, the most impervious to change, will collapse first. This has already happened in the case of Soviet Communism. How deeply entrenched, how solid and monolithic it appeared, and yet within a few years, it disintegrated from within. No one foresaw this. All were taken by surprise. There are many more such surprises in store for us.

## THE URGENCY OF TRANSFORMATION

When faced with a radical crisis, when the old way of being in the world, of interacting with each other and with the realm of nature doesn't work anymore, when survival is threatened by seemingly insurmountable problems, an individual life-form—or a species—will either die or become extinct or rise above the limitations of its condition through an evolutionary leap.

It is believed that the life-forms on this planet first evolved in the sea. When there were no animals yet to be found on land, the sea was already teeming with life. Then at some point, one of the sea creatures must have started to venture onto dry land. It would perhaps crawl a few inches at first, then, exhausted by the enormous gravitational pull of the planet, it would return to the water, where gravity is almost nonexistent and where it could live with much greater ease. And then it tried again and again and again, and much later would adapt to life on land, grow feet instead of fins, develop lungs instead of gills. It seems unlikely that a species would venture into such an alien environment and undergo an evolutionary transformation unless it was compelled to do so by some crisis situation. There may have been a large sea area that got cut off from the main ocean where the water gradually receded over thousands of years, forcing fish to leave their habitat and evolve.

Responding to a radical crisis that threatens our very survival—this is humanity's challenge now. The dysfunction of the egoic human mind, recognized already more than 2,500 years ago by the ancient wisdom teachers and now magnified through science and technology, is for the first time threatening the survival of the planet. Until very recently, the transformation of human consciousness—also pointed to by the ancient teachers—was no more than a possibility, realized by a few rare individuals here and there, irrespective of cultural or religious background. A widespread flowering of human consciousness did not happen because it was not yet imperative.

A significant portion of the earth's population will soon recognize, if they haven't already done so, that humanity is now faced with a stark choice: Evolve or die. A still relatively small but rapidly growing percentage of humanity is already experiencing within themselves the breakup of the old egoic mind patterns and the emergence of a new dimension of consciousness.

What is arising now is not a new belief system, a new religion, spiritual ideology, or mythology. We are coming to the end not only of mythologies but also of ideologies and belief systems. The change goes deeper than the content of your mind, deeper than your thoughts. In fact, at the heart of the new consciousness lies the transcendence of thought, the newfound ability of rising above thought, of realizing a dimension within yourself that is infinitely more vast than thought. You then no longer derive your identity, your sense of who you are, from the incessant stream of thinking that in the old consciousness you take to be yourself. What a liberation to realize that the "voice in my head" is not who I am. Who am I then? The one who sees that. The awareness that is prior to thought, the space in which the thought—or the emotion or sense perception—happens.

Ego is no more than this: identification with form, which primarily means thought forms. If evil has any reality—and it has a relative, not an absolute, reality—this is also its definition: complete identification with form—physical forms, thought forms, emotional forms. This results in a total unawareness of my connectedness with the whole, my intrinsic oneness with every "other" as well as with the Source. This forgetfulness is original sin, suffering, delusion. When this delusion of utter separateness underlies and governs whatever I think, say, and do, what kind of world do I create? To find the answer to this, observe how humans relate to each other, read a history book, or watch the news on television tonight.

If the structures of the human mind remain unchanged, we will always end up re-creating fundamentally the same world, the same evils, the same dysfunction.

## A NEW HEAVEN AND A NEW EARTH

The inspiration for the title of this book came from a Bible prophecy that seems more applicable now than at any other time in human history. It occurs in both the Old and the New Testament and speaks of the collapse of the existing world order and the arising of "a new heaven and a new earth."[1] We need to understand here that heaven is not a location but refers to the inner realm of consciousness. This is the esoteric meaning of the word, and this is also its meaning in the teachings of Jesus. Earth, on the other hand, is the outer manifestation in form, which is always a reflection of the inner. Collective human consciousness and life on our planet are intrinsically connected. *"A new heaven" is the emergence of a transformed state of human consciousness, and "a new earth" is its reflection in the physical realm.* Since human life and human consciousness are intrinsically one with the life of the planet, as the old consciousness dissolves, there are bound to be synchronistic geographic and climatic natural upheavals in many parts of the planet, some of which we are already witnessing now.

## CHAPTER TWO

# Ego: The Current State of Humanity

Words, no matter whether they are vocalized and made into sounds or remain unspoken as thoughts, can cast an almost hypnotic spell upon you. You easily lose yourself in them, become hypnotized into implicitly believing that when you have attached a word to something, you know what it is. The fact is: You don't know what it is. You have only covered up the mystery with a label. Everything, a bird, a tree, even a simple stone, and certainly a human being, is ultimately unknowable. This is because it has unfathomable depth. All we can perceive, experience, think about, is the surface layer of reality, less than the tip of an iceberg.

Underneath the surface appearance, everything is not only connected with everything else, but also with the

Source of all life out of which it came. Even a stone, and more easily a flower or a bird, could show you the way back to God, to the Source, to yourself. When you look at it or hold it and *let it be* without imposing a word or mental label on it, a sense of awe, of wonder, arises within you. Its essence silently communicates itself to you and reflects your own essence back to you. This is what great artists sense and succeed in conveying in their art. Van Gogh didn't say: "That's just an old chair." He looked, and looked, and looked. He sensed the Beingness of the chair. Then he sat in front of the canvas and took up the brush. The chair itself would have sold for the equivalent of a few dollars. The painting of that same chair today would fetch in excess of $25 million.

When you don't cover up the world with words and labels, a sense of the miraculous returns to your life that was lost a long time ago when humanity, instead of using thought, became possessed by thought. A depth returns to your life. Things regain their newness, their freshness. And the greatest miracle is the experiencing of your essential self as prior to any words, thoughts, mental labels, and images. For this to happen, you need to disentangle your sense of I, of Beingness, from all the things it has become mixed up with, that is to say, identified with. That disentanglement is what this book is about.

The quicker you are in attaching verbal or mental labels to things, people, or situations, the more shallow and lifeless your reality becomes, and the more deadened you become to reality, the miracle of life that continuously unfolds within and around you. In this way, cleverness may be gained, but wisdom is lost, and so are joy, love, creativity, and aliveness. They are concealed in the still gap between the perception and the interpretation. Of course we have to use words and thoughts. They have their own beauty— but do we need to become imprisoned in them?

Words reduce reality to something the human mind can grasp, which isn't very much. Language consists of five basic sounds produced by the vocal cords. They are the vowels *a, e, i, o, u.* The other sounds are consonants produced by air pressure: *s, f, g,* and so forth. Do you believe some combination of such basic sounds could ever explain who you are, or the ultimate purpose of the universe, or even what a tree or stone is in its depth?

## THE ILLUSORY SELF

The word "I" embodies the greatest error and the deepest truth, depending on how it is used. In conventional usage, it is not only one of the most frequently used words in the language (together with the related words: "me," "my," "mine," and "myself") but also one of the most misleading. In normal everyday usage, "I" embodies the primordial error, a misperception of who you are, an illusory sense of identity. This is the ego. This illusory sense of self is what Albert Einstein, who had deep insights not only into the reality of space and time but also into human nature, referred to as "an optical illusion of consciousness." That illusory self then becomes the basis for all further interpretations, or rather misinterpretations of reality, all thought processes, interactions, and relationships. Your reality becomes a reflection of the original illusion.

The good news is: If you can recognize illusion as illusion, it dissolves. The recognition of illusion is also its ending. Its survival depends on your mistaking it for reality. In the seeing of who you are not, the reality of who you are emerges by itself. This is what happens as you slowly and carefully read this and the next chapter, which are about the mechanics of the false self we call the ego. So what is the nature of this illusory self?

What you usually refer to when you say "I" is not who you are. By a monstrous act of reductionism, the infinite depth of who you are is confused with a sound produced by the vocal cords or the thought of "I" in your mind and whatever the "I" has identified with. So what do the usual "I" and the related "me," "my," or "mine" refer to?

When a young child learns that a sequence of sounds produced by the parents' vocal cords is his or her name, the child begins to equate a word, which in the mind becomes a thought, with who he or she is. At that stage, some children refer to themselves in the third person. "Johnny is hungry." Soon after, they learn the magic word "I" and cquate it with their name, which they have already equated with who they are. Then other thoughts come and merge with the original I-thought. The next step are thoughts of me and mine to designate things that are somehow part of "I." This is identification with objects, which means investing *things*, but ultimately thoughts that represent things, with a sense of self, thereby deriving an identity from them. When "my" toy breaks or is taken away, intense suffering arises. Not because of any intrinsic value that the toy has—the child will soon lose interest in it, and it will be replaced by other toys, other objects—but because of the thought of "mine." The toy became part of the child's developing sense of self, of "I."

And so as the child grows up, the original I-thought attracts other thoughts to itself: It becomes identified with a gender, possessions, the sense-perceived body, a nationality, race, religion, profession. Other things the "I" identifies with are roles—mother, father, husband, wife, and so on—accumulated knowledge or opinions, likes and dislikes, and also things that happened to "me" in the past, the memory of which are thoughts that further define my sense of self as "me and my story." These are only some of the things people derive their sense of identity from. They are ultimately no more than thoughts held together precariously by the fact that they are all invested with a sense of self. This mental construct is what you normally refer to when you say "I." To be more precise: Most of the time it is not you who speaks when you say or think "I" but some aspect of that mental construct, the egoic self. Once you awaken, you still use the word "I," but it will come from a much deeper place within yourself.

Most people are still completely identified with the incessant stream of mind, of compulsive thinking, most of it repetitive and pointless. There is no "I" apart from their thought processes and the emotions that go with them. This is the meaning of being spiritually unconscious. When told that there is a voice in their head that never stops speaking, they say, "What voice?" or angrily deny it, which of course *is* the voice, is the thinker, is the unobserved mind. It could almost be looked upon as an entity that has taken possession of them.

Some people never forget the first time they disidentified from their thoughts and thus briefly experienced the shift in identity from being the content of their mind to being the awareness in the background. For others it happens in such a subtle way they hardly notice it, or they just notice an influx of joy or inner peace without knowing the reason.

## THE VOICE IN THE HEAD

That first glimpse of awareness came to me when I was a first-year student at the University of London. I would take the tube (subway) twice a week to go to the university library, usually around nine o'clock in the morning, toward the end of the rush hour. One time a woman in her early thirties sat opposite me. I had seen her before a few times on that train. One could not help but notice her. Although the train was full, the seats on either side of her were unoccupied, the reason being, no doubt, that she appeared to be quite insane. She looked extremely tense and talked to herself incessantly in a loud and angry voice. She was so absorbed in her thoughts that she was totally unaware, it seemed, of other people or her surroundings. Her head was facing downward and slightly to the left, as if she were addressing someone sitting in the empty seat next to her. Although I don't remember the precise content, her monologue went something like this: "And then she said to me . . . so I said to her you are a liar how dare you accuse me of . . . when you are the one who has always taken advantage of me I trusted you and you betrayed my trust. . . ." There was the angry tone in her voice of someone who has been wronged, who needs to defend her position lest she become annihilated.

As the train approached Tottenham Court Road Station, she stood up and walked toward the door with still no break in the stream of words coming out of her mouth. That was my stop too, so I got off behind her. At street level, she began to walk toward Bedford Square, still engaged in her imaginary dialogue, still angrily accusing and asserting her position. My curiosity aroused, I decided to follow her as long as she was walking in the same general direction I had to go in. Although engrossed in her imaginary dialogue, she seemed to know where she was going. Soon we were within sight of the imposing structure of Senate House, a 1930s high-rise, the university's central administrative building and library. I was shocked. Was it possible that we were going to the same place? Yes, that's where she was heading. Was she a teacher, a student, an office worker, a librarian? Maybe she was some psychologist's research project. I never knew the answer. I walked twenty steps behind her, and by the time I entered the building (which ironically was the location of the headquarters of the "Mind Police" in the film version of George Orwell's novel, *1984*), she had already been swallowed up by one of the elevators.

I was somewhat taken aback by what I had just witnessed. A mature first-year student at twenty-five, I saw myself as an intellectual in the making, and I was convinced that all the answers to the dilemmas of human existence could be found through the intellect, that is to say, by thinking. I didn't realize yet that thinking without awareness *is* the main dilemma of human existence. I looked upon the professors as sages who had all the answers and upon the university as the temple of knowledge. How could an insane person like her be part of this?

I was still thinking about her when I was in the men's room prior to entering the library. As I was washing my hands, I thought: I hope I don't end up like her. The man next to me looked briefly in my direction, and I suddenly was shocked when I realized that I hadn't just thought those words, but mumbled them aloud. "Oh my God, I'm already like her," I thought. Wasn't my mind as incessantly active as hers? There were only minor differences between us. The predominant underlying emotion behind her thinking seemed to be anger. In my case, it was mostly anxiety. She thought out loud. I thought—mostly—in my head. If she was mad, then everyone was mad, including myself. There were differences in degree only.

For a moment, I was able to stand back from my own mind and see it from a deeper perspective, as it were. There was a brief shift from thinking to awareness. I was still in the men's room, but alone now, looking at my face in the mirror. At that moment of detachment from my mind, I laughed out loud. It may have sounded insane, but it was the laughter of sanity, the laughter of the big-bellied Buddha. "Life isn't as serious as my mind makes it out to be." That's what the laughter seemed to be saying. But it was only a glimpse, very quickly to be forgotten. I would spend the next three years in anxiety and depression, completely identified with my mind. I had to get close to suicide before awareness returned, and then it was much more than a glimpse. I became free of compulsive thinking and of the false, mind-made I.

The above incident not only gave me a first glimpse of

awareness, it also planted the first doubt as to the absolute validity of the human intellect. A few months later, something tragic happened that made my doubt grow. On a Monday morning, we arrived for a lecture to be given by a professor whose mind I admired greatly, only to be told that sadly he had committed suicide sometime during the weekend by shooting himself. I was stunned. He was a highly respected teacher and seemed to have all the answers. However, I could as yet see no alternative to the cultivation of thought. I didn't realize yet that thinking is only a tiny aspect of the consciousness that we are, nor did I know anything about the ego, let alone being able to detect it within myself.

## CONTENT AND STRUCTURE OF THE EGO

The egoic mind is completely conditioned by the past. Its conditioning is twofold: It consists of content and structure.

In the case of a child who cries in deep suffering because his toy has been taken away, the toy represents content. It is interchangeable with any other content, any other toy or object. The content you identify with is conditioned by your environment, your upbringing, and surrounding culture. Whether the child is rich or poor, whether the toy is a piece of wood shaped like an animal or a sophisticated electronic gadget makes no difference as far as the suffering caused by its loss is concerned. The reason why such acute suffering occurs is concealed in the word "my," and it is structural. The unconscious compulsion to enhance one's identity through association with an object is built into the very structure of the egoic mind.

One of the most basic mind structures through which the ego comes into existence is identification. The word "identification" is derived from the Latin word *idem*, meaning "same" and *facere*, which means "to make." So when I identify with something, I "make it the same." The same as what? The same as I. I endow it with a sense of self, and so it becomes part of my "identity." One of the most basic levels of identification is with things: My toy later becomes my car, my house, my clothes, and so on. I try to find myself in things but never quite make it and end up losing myself in them. That is the fate of the ego.

## IDENTIFICATION WITH THINGS

The people in the advertising industry know very well that in order to sell things that people don't really need, they must convince them that those things will add something to how they see themselves or are seen by others; in other words, add something to their sense of self. They do this, for example, by telling you that you will stand out from the crowd by using this product and so by implication be more fully yourself. Or they may create an association in your mind between the product and a famous person, or a youthful, attractive, or happy-looking person. Even pictures of old or deceased celebrities in their prime work well for that purpose. The unspoken assumption is that by buying this product, through some magical act of appropriation, you become like them, or rather the surface image of them. And so in many cases you are not buying a product but an "identity enhancer." Designer labels are primarily collective identities that you buy into. They are expensive and therefore "exclusive." If everybody could buy them, they would lose their psychological value and all you would be left with would be their material value, which likely amounts to a fraction of what you paid.

What kind of things you identify with will vary from person to person according to age, gender, income, social class, fashion, the surrounding culture, and so on. *What* you identify with is all to do with content; whereas, the unconscious compulsion to identify is structural. It is one of the most basic ways in which the egoic mind operates.

Paradoxically, what keeps the so-called consumer society going is the fact that trying to find yourself through things doesn't work: The ego satisfaction is short-lived and so you keep looking for more, keep buying, keep consuming.

Of course, in this physical dimension that our surface selves inhabit, things are a necessary and inescapable part of our lives. We need housing, clothes, furniture, tools, transportation. There may also be things in our lives that we value because of their beauty or inherent quality. We need to honor the world of things, not despise it. Each thing has Beingness, is a temporary form that has its origin within the formless one Life, the source of all things, all bodies, all forms. In most ancient cultures, people believed that everything, even so-called inanimate objects, had an indwelling spirit, and in this respect they were closer to the truth than we are today. When you live in a world deadened by mental abstraction, you don't sense the aliveness of the universe anymore. Most people don't inhabit a living reality, but a conceptualized one.

But we cannot really honor things if we use them as a means to self-enhancement, that is to say, if we try to find ourselves through them. This is exactly what the ego does. Ego-identification with things creates attachment to things, obsession with things, which in turn creates our consumer society and economic structures where the only measure of progress is always *more*. The unchecked striving for more, for endless growth, is a dysfunction and a disease. It is the same dysfunction the cancerous cell manifests, whose only goal is to multiply itself, unaware that it is bringing about its own destruction by destroying the organism of which it is a part. Some economists are so attached to the notion of growth that they can't let go of that word, so they refer to recession as a time of "negative growth."

A large part of many people's lives is consumed by an obsessive preoccupation with things. This is why one of the ills of our times is object proliferation. When you can no longer feel the life that you are, you are likely to try to fill up your life with things. As a spiritual practice, I suggest that you investigate your relationship with the world of things through self-observation, and in particular, things that are designated with the word "my." You need to be alert and honest to find out, for example, whether your sense of self-worth is bound up with things you possess. Do certain things induce a subtle feeling of importance or superiority? Does the lack of them make you feel inferior to others who have more than you? Do you casually mention things you own or show them off to increase your sense of worth in someone else's eyes and through them in your own? Do you feel resentful or angry and somehow diminished in your sense of self when someone else has more than you or when you lose a prized possession?

## THE LOST RING

When I was seeing people as a counselor and spiritual teacher, I would visit a woman twice a week whose body was riddled with cancer. She was a schoolteacher in her midforties and had been given no more than a few months to live by her doctors. Sometimes a few words were spoken during those visits, but mostly we would sit together in silence, and as we did, she had her first glimpses of the stillness within herself that she never knew existed during her busy life as a schoolteacher.

One day, however, I arrived to find her in a state of great distress and anger. "What happened?" I asked. Her diamond ring, of great monetary as well as sentimental value, had disappeared, and she said she was sure it had been stolen by the woman who came to look after her for a few hours every day. She said she didn't understand how anybody could be so callous and heartless as to do this to her. She asked me whether she should confront the woman or whether it would be better to call the police immediately. I said I couldn't tell her what to do, but asked her to find out how important a ring or anything else was at this point in her life. "You don't understand," she said. "This was my grandmother's ring. I used to wear it every day until I got ill and my hands became too swollen. It's more than just a ring to me. How can I not be upset?"

The quickness of her response and the anger and defensiveness in her voice were indications that she had not yet become present enough to look within and to disentangle her reaction from the event and observe them both. Her anger and defensiveness were signs that the ego was still speaking through her. I said, "I am going to ask you a few questions, but instead of answering them now, see if you can find the answers within you. I will pause briefly after each question. When an answer comes, it may not necessarily come in the form of words." She said she was ready to listen. I asked: "Do you realize that you will have to let go of the ring at some point, perhaps quite soon? How much more time do you need before you will be ready to let go of it? Will you become less when you let go of it? Has *who you are* become diminished by the loss?" There were a few minutes of silence after the last question.

When she started speaking again, there was a smile on her face, and she seemed at peace. "The last question made me realize something important. First I went to my mind for an answer and my mind said, 'Yes, of course you have been diminished.' Then I asked myself the question again, 'Has who I am become diminished?' This time I tried to feel rather than think the answer. And suddenly I could feel my I Am-ness. I have never felt that before. If I can feel the I Am so strongly, then who I am hasn't been diminished at all. I can still feel it now, something peaceful but very alive."

"That is the joy of Being," I said. "You can only feel it when you get out of your head. Being must be felt. It can't be thought. The ego doesn't know about it because thought is what it consists of. The ring was really in your head as a thought that you confused with the sense of I Am. You thought the I Am or a part of it was in the ring.

"Whatever the ego seeks and gets attached to are substitutes for the Being that it cannot feel. You can value and care for things, but whenever you get attached to them, you will know it's the ego. And you are never really attached to a thing but to a thought that has 'I,' 'me,' or 'mine' in it. Whenever you completely accept a loss, you go beyond ego, and who you are, the I Am which is consciousness itself, emerges."

She said, "Now I understand something Jesus said that never made much sense to me before: 'If someone takes your shirt, let him have your coat as well.' "

"That's right," I said. "It doesn't mean you should never lock your door. All it means is that sometimes letting things go is an act of far greater power than defending or hanging on."

In the last few weeks of her life as her body became weaker, she became more and more radiant, as if light were shining through her. She gave many of her possessions away, some to the woman she thought had stolen the ring, and with each thing she gave away, her joy deepened. When her mother called me to let me know she had passed away, she also mentioned that after her death they found her ring in the medicine cabinet in the bathroom. Did the woman return the ring, or had it been there all the time? Nobody will ever know. One thing we do know: Life will give you whatever experience is most helpful for the evolution of your consciousness. How do you know this is the experience you need? Because this is the experience you are having at this moment.

Is it wrong then to be proud of one's possessions or to feel resentful toward people who have more than you? Not at all. That sense of pride, of needing to stand out, the apparent enhancement of one's self through "more than" and diminishment through "less than" is neither right nor wrong—it is the ego. The ego isn't wrong; it's just unconscious. When you observe the ego in yourself, you are beginning to go beyond it. Don't take the ego too seriously. When you detect egoic behavior in yourself, smile. At times you may even laugh. How could humanity have been taken in by this for so long? Above all, know that the ego isn't personal. It isn't who you are. If you consider the ego to be your personal problem, that's just more ego.

## THE ILLUSION OF OWNERSHIP

To "own" something—what does it really mean? What does it mean to make something "mine"? If you stand on a street in New York, point to a huge skyscraper and say, "That building is mine. I own it," you are either very wealthy or you are delusional or a liar. In any case, you are telling a story in which the thought form "I" and the thought form "building" merge into one. That's how the mental concept of ownership works. If everybody agrees with your story, there will be signed pieces of paper to certify their agreement with it. You are wealthy. If nobody agrees with the story, they will send you to a psychiatrist. You are delusional, or a compulsive liar.

It is important to recognize here that the story and the thought forms that make up the story, whether people agree with it or not, have absolutely nothing to do with who you are. Even if people agree with it, it is ultimately a fiction. Many people don't realize until they are on their deathbed and everything external falls away that *no thing* ever had anything to do with who they are. In the proximity of death, the whole concept of ownership stands revealed as ultimately meaningless. In the last moments of their life, they then also realize that while they were looking throughout their lives for a more complete sense of self, what they were really looking for, their Being, had actually always already been there, but had been largely obscured by their identification with things, which ultimately means identification with their mind.

"Blessed are the poor in spirit," Jesus said, "for theirs will be the kingdom of heaven."[1] What does "poor in spirit" mean? No inner baggage, no identifications. Not with things, nor with any mental concepts that have a sense of self in them. And what is the "kingdom of heaven"? The simple but profound joy of Being that is there when you let go of identifications and so become "poor in spirit."

This is why renouncing all possessions has been an ancient spiritual practice in both East and West. Renunciation of possessions, however, will not automatically free you of the ego. It will attempt to ensure its survival by finding something else to identify with, for example, a mental image of yourself as someone who has transcended all interest in material possessions and is therefore superior, is *more*

spiritual than others. There are people who have re-
nounced all possessions but have a bigger ego than some
millionaires. If you take away one kind of identification,
the ego will quickly find another. It ultimately doesn't
mind what it identifies with as long as it has an identity.
Anticonsumerism or antiprivate ownership would be another thought form, another mental position, that can replace identification with possessions. Through it you could
make yourself right and others wrong. As we shall see later,
making yourself right and others wrong is one of the prin-
cipal egoic mind patterns, one of the main forms of unconsciousness. In other words, the content of the ego may
change; the mind structure that keeps it alive does not.

One of the unconscious assumptions is that by identifying with an object through the fiction of ownership, the
apparent solidity and permanency of that material object
will endow your sense of self with greater solidity and permanency. This applies particularly to buildings and even
more so to land since it is the only thing you think you can
own that cannot be destroyed. The absurdity of owning
something becomes even more apparent in the case of land.
In the days of the white settlement, the natives of North
America found ownership of land an incomprehensible
concept. And so they lost it when the Europeans made
them sign pieces of paper that were equally incomprehensible to them. They felt they belonged to the land, but the
land did not belong to them.

The ego tends to equate having with Being: I have, therefore I am. And the more I have, the more I am. The ego lives through comparison. How you are seen by others turns into how you see yourself. If everyone lived in a mansion or everyone was wealthy, your mansion or your wealth would no longer serve to enhance your sense of self. You could then move to a simple cabin, give up your wealth, and regain an identity by seeing yourself and being seen as more spiritual than others. How you are seen by others becomes the mirror that tells you what you are like and who you are. The ego's sense of self-worth is in most cases bound up with the worth you have in the eyes of others. You need others to give you a sense of self, and if you live in a culture that to a large extent equates self-worth with how much and what you have, if you cannot look through this collective delusion, you will be condemned to chasing after things for the rest of your life in the vain hope of finding your worth and completion of your sense of self there.

How do you let go of attachment to things? Don't even try. It's impossible. Attachment to things drops away by itself when you no longer seek to find yourself in them. In the meantime, just be aware of your attachment to things. Sometimes you may not know that you are attached to something, which is to say, identified, until you lose it or there is the threat of loss. If you then become upset, anxious, and so on, it means you are attached. If you are aware that you are identified with a thing, the identification is no longer total. "I am the awareness that is aware that there is attachment." That's the beginning of the transformation of consciousness.

## WANTING: THE NEED FOR MORE

The ego identifies with having, but its satisfaction in having is a relatively shallow and short-lived one. Concealed within it remains a deep-seated sense of dissatisfaction, of incompleteness, of "not enough." "I don't have enough yet," by which the ego really means, "I *am* not enough yet."

As we have seen, *having*—the concept of ownership—is a fiction created by the ego to give itself solidity and permanency and make itself stand out, make itself special. Since you cannot find yourself through having, however, there is another more powerful drive underneath it that pertains to the structure of the ego: the need for more, which we could also call "wanting." No ego can last for long without the need for more. Therefore, wanting keeps the ego alive much more than having. The ego wants to want more than it wants to have. And so the shallow satisfaction of having is always replaced by more wanting. This is the psychological need for more, that is to say, more things to identify with. It is an addictive need, not an authentic one.

In some cases, the psychological need for more or the feeling of not enough that is so characteristic of the ego becomes transferred to the physical level and so turns into insatiable hunger. The sufferers of bulimia will often make themselves vomit so they can continue eating. Their mind is hungry, not their body. This eating disorder would become healed if the sufferers, instead of being identified with their mind, could get in touch with their body and so feel the true needs of the body rather than the pseudo-needs of the egoic mind.

Some egos know what they want and pursue their aim with grim and ruthless determination—Genghis Khan, Stalin, Hitler, to give just a few larger-than-life examples. The energy behind their wanting, however, creates an opposing energy of equal intensity that in the end leads to their downfall. In the meantime, they make themselves and many others unhappy, or, in the larger-than-life examples, create hell on earth. Most egos have conflicting wants. They want different things at different times or may not even know what they want except that they don't want what is: the present moment. Unease, restlessness, boredom, anxiety, dissatisfaction, are the result of unfulfilled wanting. Wanting is structural, so no amount of content can provide lasting fulfillment as long as that mental structure remains in place. Intense wanting that has no specific object can often be found in the still-developing ego of teenagers, some of whom are in a permanent state of negativity and dissatisfaction.

The physical needs for food, water, shelter, clothing, and

basic comforts could be easily met for all humans on the planet, were it not for the imbalance of resources created by the insane and rapacious need for more, the greed of the ego. It finds collective expression in the economic structures of this world, such as the huge corporations, which are egoic entities that compete with each other for more. Their only blind aim is profit. They pursue that aim with absolute ruthlessness. Nature, animals, people, even their own employees, are no more than digits on a balance sheet, lifeless objects to be used, then discarded.

The thought forms of "me" and "mine," of "more than," of "I want," "I need," "I must have," and of "not enough" pertain not to content but to the structure of the ego. The content is interchangeable. As long as you don't recognize those thought forms within yourself, as long as they remain unconscious, you will believe in what they say; you will be condemned to acting out those unconscious thoughts, condemned to seeking and not finding—because when those thought forms operate, no possession, place, person, or condition will ever satisfy you. No content will satisfy you, as long as the egoic structure remains in place. No matter what you have or get, you won't be happy. You will always be looking for something else that promises greater fulfillment, that promises to make your incomplete sense of self complete and fill that sense of lack you feel within.

## IDENTIFICATION WITH THE BODY

Apart from objects, another basic form of identification is with "my" body. Firstly, the body is male or female, and so the sense of being a man or woman takes up a significant part of most people's sense of self. Gender becomes identity. Identification with gender is encouraged at an early age, and it forces you into a role, into conditioned patterns of behavior that affect all aspects of your life, not just sexuality. It is a role many people become completely trapped in, even more so in some of the traditional societies than in Western culture where identification with gender is beginning to lessen somewhat. In some traditional cultures, the worst fate a woman can have is to be unwed or barren, and for a man to lack sexual potency and not be able to produce children. Life's fulfillment is perceived to be fulfillment of one's gender identity.

In the West, it is the physical appearance of the body that contributes greatly to the sense of who you think you are: its strength or weakness, its perceived beauty or ugliness relative to others. For many people, their sense of self-worth is intimately bound up with their physical strength, good looks, fitness, and external appearance. Many feel a diminished sense of self-worth because they perceive their body as ugly or imperfect.

In some cases, the mental image or concept of "my body" is a complete distortion of reality. A young woman may think of herself as overweight and therefore starve herself when in fact she is quite thin. She cannot see her body anymore. All she "sees" is the mental concept of her body, which says "I am fat" or "I will become fat." At the root of this condition lies identification with the mind. As people have become more and more mind-identified, which is the intensification of egoic dysfunction, there has also been a dramatic increase in the incidence of anorexia in recent decades. If the sufferer could look at her body without the interfering judgments of her mind or even recognize those judgments for what they are instead of believing in them— or better still, if she could feel her body from within—this would initiate her healing.

Those who are identified with their good looks, physical strength, or abilities experience suffering when those attributes begin to fade and disappear, as of course they will. Their very identity that was based on them is then threatened with collapse. In either case, ugly or beautiful, people derive a significant part of their identity, be it negative or positive, from their body. To be more precise, they derive their identity from the I-thought that they erroneously attach to the mental image or concept of their body, which after all is no more than a physical form that shares the destiny of all forms—impermanence and ultimately decay.

Equating the physical sense-perceived body that is destined to grow old, wither, and die with "I" always leads to suffering sooner or later. To refrain from identifying with the body doesn't mean that you neglect, despise, or no longer care for it. If it is strong, beautiful, or vigorous, you can enjoy and appreciate those attributes—while they last. You can also improve the body's condition through right nutrition and exercise. If you don't equate the body with who you are, when beauty fades, vigor diminishes, or the body becomes incapacitated, this will not affect your sense of worth or identity in any way. In fact, as the body begins to weaken, the formless dimension, the light of consciousness, can shine more easily through the fading form.

It is not just people with good or near-perfect bodies who are likely to equate it with who they are. You can just as easily identify with a "problematic" body and make the body's imperfection, illness, or disability into your identity. You may then think and speak of yourself as a "sufferer" of this or that chronic illness or disability. You receive a great deal of attention from doctors and others who constantly confirm to you your conceptual identity as a sufferer or a patient. You then unconsciously cling to the illness because it has become the most important part of who you perceive yourself to be. It has become another thought form with which the ego can identify. Once the ego has found an identity, it does not want to let go. Amazingly but not infrequently, the ego in search of a stronger identity can and does create illnesses in order to strengthen itself through them.

## FEELING THE INNER BODY

Although body-identification is one of the most basic forms of ego, the good news is that it is also the one that you can most easily go beyond. This is done not by trying to convince yourself that you are not your body, but by shifting your attention from the external form of your body and from thoughts about your body—beautiful, ugly, strong, weak, too fat, too thin—to the feeling of aliveness inside it. No matter what your body's appearance is on the outer level, beyond the outer form it is an intensely alive energy field.

If you are not familiar with "inner body" awareness, close your eyes for a moment and find out if there is life inside your hands. Don't ask your mind. It will say, "I can't feel anything." Probably it will also say, "Give me something more interesting to think about." So instead of asking your mind, go to the hands directly. By this I mean become aware of the subtle feeling of aliveness inside them. It is there. You just have to go there with your attention to notice it. You may get a slight tingling sensation at first, then a feeling of energy or aliveness. If you hold your attention in your hands for a while, the sense of aliveness will intensify. Some people won't even have to close their eyes. They will be able to feel their "inner hands" at the same time as they read this. Then go to your feet, keep your attention there for a minute or so, and begin to feel your hands and feet at the same time. Then incorporate other parts of the body—legs, arms, abdomen, chest, and so on—into that feeling until you are aware of the inner body as a global sense of aliveness.

What I call the "inner body" isn't really the body anymore but life energy, the bridge between form and formlessness. Make it a habit to feel the inner body as often as you can. After a while, you won't need to close your eyes anymore to feel it. For example, see if you can feel the inner body whenever you listen to someone. It almost seems like a paradox: When you are in touch with the inner body, you are not identified with your body anymore, nor are you identified with your mind. This is to say, you are no longer identified with form but moving away from form-identification toward formlessness, which we may also call Being. It is your essence identity. Body awareness not only anchors you in the present moment, it is a doorway out of the prison that is the ego. It also strengthens the immune system and the body's ability to heal itself.

## FORGETFULNESS OF BEING

Ego is always identification with form, seeking yourself and thereby losing yourself in some form. Forms are not just material objects and physical bodies. More fundamental than the external forms—things and bodies—are the thought forms that continuously arise in the field of consciousness.

They are energy formations, finer and less dense than physical matter, but they are forms nonetheless. What you may be aware of as a voice in your head that never stops speaking is the stream of incessant and compulsive thinking. When every thought absorbs your attention completely, when you are so identified with the voice in your head and the emotions that accompany it that you lose yourself in every thought and every emotion, then you are totally identified with form and therefore in the grip of ego. Ego is a conglomeration of recurring thought forms and conditioned mental-emotional patterns that are invested with a sense of I, a sense of self. Ego arises when your sense of Beingness, of "I Am," which is formless consciousness, gets mixed up with form. This is the meaning of identification. This is forgetfulness of Being, the primary error, the illusion of absolute separateness that turns reality into a nightmare.

## FROM DESCARTES'S ERROR TO SARTRE'S INSIGHT

The seventeenth-century philosopher Descartes, regarded as the founder of modern philosophy, gave expression to this primary error with his famous dictum (which he saw as primary truth): "I think, therefore I am." This was the answer he found to the question "Is there anything I can know with absolute certainty?" He realized that the fact that he was always thinking was beyond doubt, and so he equated thinking with Being, that is to say, identity—I am—with thinking. Instead of the ultimate truth, he had found the root of the ego, but he didn't know that.

It took almost three hundred years before another famous philosopher saw something in that statement that Descartes, as well as everybody else, had overlooked. His name was Jean-Paul Sartre. He looked at Descartes's statement "I think, therefore I am" very deeply and suddenly realized, in his own words, "The consciousness that says 'I am' is not the consciousness that thinks." What did he mean by that? When you are aware that you are thinking, that awareness is not part of thinking. It is a different dimension of consciousness. And it is that awareness that says "I am." If there were nothing but thought in you, you wouldn't even know you are thinking. You would be like a dreamer who doesn't know he is dreaming. You would be as identified with every thought as the dreamer is with every image in the dream. Many people still live like that, like sleepwalkers, trapped in old dysfunctional mind-sets that continuously re-create the same nightmarish reality. When you know you are dreaming, you are awake within the dream. Another dimension of consciousness has come in.

The implication of Sartre's insight is profound, but he himself was still too identified with thinking to realize the full significance of what he had discovered: an emerging new dimension of consciousness.

## THE PEACE THAT PASSES
## ALL UNDERSTANDING

There are many accounts of people who experienced that emerging new dimension of consciousness as a result of tragic loss at some point in their lives. Some lost all of their possessions, others their children or spouse, their social position, reputation, or physical abilities. In some cases, through disaster or war, they lost all of these simultaneously and found themselves with "nothing." We may call this a limit-situation. Whatever they had identified with, whatever gave them their sense of self, had been taken away. Then suddenly and inexplicably, the anguish or intense fear they initially felt gave way to a sacred sense of Presence, a deep peace and serenity and complete freedom from fear. This phenomenon must have been familiar to St. Paul, who used the expression "the peace of God which passeth all understanding."[2] It is indeed a peace that doesn't seem to make sense, and the people who experienced it asked themselves: In the face of *this*, how can it be that I feel such peace?

The answer is simple, once you realize what the ego is and how it works. When forms that you had identified with, that gave you your sense of self, collapse or are taken away, it can lead to a collapse of the ego, since ego *is* identification with form. When there is nothing to identify with anymore, who are you? When forms around you die or death approaches, your sense of Beingness, of I Am, is freed from its entanglement with form: Spirit is released from its imprisonment in matter. You realize your essential identity as formless, as an all-pervasive Presence, of Being prior to all forms, all identifications. You realize your true identity as consciousness itself, rather than what consciousness had identified with. That's the peace of God. The ultimate truth of who you are is not I am this or I am that, but I Am.

Not everybody who experiences great loss also experiences this awakening, this disidentification from form. Some immediately create a strong mental image or thought form in which they see themselves as a victim, whether it be of circumstances, other people, an unjust fate, or God. This thought form and the emotions it creates, such as anger, resentment, self-pity, and so on, they strongly identify with, and it immediately takes the place of all the other identifications that have collapsed through the loss. In other words, the ego quickly finds a new form. The fact that this new form is a deeply unhappy one doesn't concern the ego too much, as long as it has an identity, good or bad. In fact, this new ego will be more contracted, more rigid and impenetrable than the old one.

Whenever tragic loss occurs, you either resist or you yield. Some people become bitter or deeply resentful; others become compassionate, wise, and loving. Yielding means inner acceptance of what is. You are open to life.

Resistance is an inner contraction, a hardening of the shell of the ego. You are closed. Whatever action you take in a state of inner resistance (which we could also call negativity) will create more outer resistance, and the universe will not be on your side; life will not be helpful. If the shutters are closed, the sunlight cannot come in. When you yield internally, when you surrender, a new dimension of consciousness opens up. If action is possible or necessary, your action will be in alignment with the whole and supported by creative intelligence, the unconditioned consciousness which in a state of inner openness you become one with. Circumstances and people then become helpful, cooperative. Coincidences happen. If no action is possible, you rest in the peace and inner stillness that come with surrender. You rest in God.

CHAPTER THREE

# The Core of Ego

Most people are so completely identified with the voice in the head—the incessant stream of involuntary and compulsive thinking and the emotions that accompany it—that we may describe them as being possessed by their mind. As long as you are completely unaware of this, you take the thinker to be who you are. This is the egoic mind. We call it egoic because there is a sense of self, of I (ego), in every thought—every memory, every interpretation, opinion, viewpoint, reaction, emotion. This is unconsciousness, spiritually speaking. Your thinking, the content of your mind, is of course conditioned by the past: your upbringing, culture, family background, and so on. The central core of all your mind activity consists of certain repetitive and persistent thoughts, emotions, and reactive patterns that you identify with most strongly. This entity is the ego itself.

In most cases, when you say "I," it is the ego speaking, not you, as we have seen. It consists of thought and emotion, of a bundle of memories you identify with as "me and my story," of habitual roles you play without knowing it, of collective identifications such as nationality, religion, race, social class, or political allegiance. It also contains personal identifications, not only with possessions, but also with opinions, external appearance, long-standing resentments, or concepts of yourself as better than or not as good as others, as a success or failure.

The content of the ego varies from person to person, but in every ego the same structure operates. In other words: Egos only differ on the surface. Deep down they are all the same. In what way are they the same? They live on identification and separation. When you live through the mind-made self comprised of thought and emotion that is the ego, the basis for your identity is precarious because thought and emotion are by their very nature ephemeral, fleeting. So every ego is continuously struggling for survival, trying to protect and enlarge itself. To uphold the I-thought, it needs the opposite thought of "the other." The conceptual "I" cannot survive without the conceptual "other." The others are most other when I see them as my enemies. At one end of the scale of this unconscious egoic pattern lies the egoic compulsive habit of faultfinding and complaining about others. Jesus referred to it when he said, "Why do you see the speck that is in your brother's eye, but do not notice the log that is in your own eye?"[1] At the other end of the scale, there is physical violence between individuals and warfare between nations. In the Bible, Jesus' question remains unanswered, but the answer is, of course: Because when I criticize or condemn another, it makes me feel bigger, superior.

## COMPLAINING AND RESENTMENT

Complaining is one of the ego's favorite strategies for strengthening itself. Every complaint is a little story the mind makes up that you completely believe in. Whether you complain aloud or only in thought makes no difference. Some egos that perhaps don't have much else to identify with easily survive on complaining alone. When you are in the grip of such an ego, complaining, especially about other people, is habitual and, of course, unconscious, which means you don't know what you are doing. Applying negative mental labels to people, either to their face or more commonly when you speak about them to others or even just think about them, is often part of this pattern. Name-calling is the crudest form of such labeling and of the ego's need to be right and triumph over others: "jerk, bastard, bitch"—all definitive pronouncements that you can't argue with. On the next level down on the scale of unconsciousness, you have shouting and screaming, and not much below that, physical violence.

Resentment is the emotion that goes with complaining and the mental labeling of people and adds even more energy to the ego. Resentment means to feel bitter, indignant, aggrieved, or offended. You resent other people's greed, their dishonesty, their lack of integrity, what they are doing, what they did in the past, what they said, what they failed to do, what they should or shouldn't have done. The ego loves it. Instead of overlooking unconsciousness in others, you make it into their identity. Who is doing that? The unconsciousness in you, the ego. Sometimes the "fault" that you perceive in another isn't even there. It is a total misinterpretation, a projection by a mind conditioned to see enemies and to make itself right or superior. At other times, the fault may be there, but by focusing on it, sometimes to the exclusion of everything else, you amplify it. And what you react to in another, you strengthen in yourself.

Nonreaction to the ego in others is one of the most effective ways not only of going beyond ego in yourself but also of dissolving the collective human ego. But you can only be in a state of nonreaction if you can recognize someone's behavior as coming from the ego, as being an expression of the collective human dysfunction. When you realize it's not personal, there is no longer a compulsion to react as if it were. By not reacting to the ego, you will often be able to bring out the sanity in others, which is the unconditioned consciousness as opposed to the conditioned. At times you may have to take practical steps to protect yourself from deeply unconscious people. This you can do without making them into enemies. Your greatest protection, however, is being conscious. Somebody becomes an enemy if you personalize the unconsciousness that is the ego. Nonreaction is not weakness but strength. Another word for nonreaction is forgiveness. To forgive is to overlook, or rather to look through. You look through the ego to the sanity that is in every human being as his or her essence.

The ego loves to complain and feel resentful not only about other people but also about situations. What you can do to a person, you can also do to a situation: make it into an enemy. The implication is always: This should not be happening; I don't want to be here; I don't want to be doing this; I'm being treated unfairly. And the ego's greatest enemy of all is, of course, the present moment, which is to say, life itself.

Complaining is not to be confused with informing someone of a mistake or deficiency so that it can be put right. And to refrain from complaining doesn't necessarily mean putting up with bad quality or behavior. There is no ego in telling the waiter that your soup is cold and needs to be heated up—if you stick to the facts, which are always neutral. "How dare you serve me cold soup. . . ." That's complaining. There is a "me" here that loves to feel personally offended by the cold soup and is going to make the most of it, a "me" that enjoys making someone wrong. The complaining we are talking about is in the service of the ego, not of change. Sometimes it becomes obvious that the ego doesn't really want change so that it can go on complaining.

See if you can catch, that is to say, notice, the voice in the head, perhaps in the very moment it complains about something, and recognize it for what it is: the voice of the ego, no more than a conditioned mind-pattern, a thought. Whenever you notice that voice, you will also realize that you are not the voice, but the one who is aware of it. In fact, you are the awareness that is aware of the voice. In the background, there is the awareness. In the foreground, there is the voice, the thinker. In this way you are becoming free of the ego, free of the unobserved mind. The moment you become aware of the ego in you, it is strictly speaking no longer the ego, but just an old, conditioned mind-pattern. Ego implies unawareness. Awareness and ego cannot coexist. The old mind-pattern or mental habit may still survive and reoccur for a while because it has the momentum of thousands of years of collective human unconsciousness behind it, but every time it is recognized, it is weakened.

## REACTIVITY AND GRIEVANCES

Whereas resentment is often the emotion that goes with complaining, it may also be accompanied by a stronger emotion such as anger or some other form of upset. In this way, it becomes more highly charged energetically. Complaining then turns into reactivity, another of the ego's ways of strengthening itself. There are many people who are always waiting for the next thing to react against, to feel annoyed or disturbed about—and it never takes long before they find it. "This is an outrage," they say. "How dare you. . . ." "I resent this." They are addicted to upset and anger as others are to a drug. Through reacting against this or that they assert and strengthen their feeling of self.

A long-standing resentment is called a grievance. To carry a grievance is to be in a permanent state of "against," and that is why grievances constitute a significant part of many people's ego. Collective grievances can survive for centuries in the psyche of a nation or tribe and fuel a never-ending cycle of violence.

A grievance is a strong negative emotion connected to an event in the sometimes distant past that is being kept alive by compulsive thinking, by retelling the story in the head or out loud of "what someone did to me" or "what someone did to us." A grievance will also contaminate other areas of your life. For example, while you think about and feel your grievance, its negative emotional energy can distort your perception of an event that is happening in the present or influence the way in which you speak or behave toward someone in the present. One strong grievance is enough to contaminate large areas of your life and keep you in the grip of the ego.

It requires honesty to see whether you still harbor griev-ances, whether there is someone in your life you have not completely forgiven, an "enemy." If you do, become aware of the grievance both on the level of thought as well as emotion, that is to say, be aware of the thoughts that keep it alive, and feel the emotion that is the body's response to those thoughts. Don't try to let go of the grievance. *Trying* to let go, to forgive, does not work. Forgiveness happens naturally when you see that it has no purpose other than to strengthen a false sense of self, to keep the ego in place. The seeing is freeing. Jesus' teaching to "Forgive your ene-mies" is essentially about the undoing of one of the main egoic structures in the human mind.

The past has no power to stop you from being present now. Only your grievance about the past can do that. And what is a grievance? The baggage of old thought and emotion.

## BEING RIGHT, MAKING WRONG

Complaining as well as faultfinding and reactivity strengthen the ego's sense of boundary and separateness on which its survival depends. But they also strengthen the ego in an-other way by giving it a feeling of superiority on which it thrives. It may not be immediately apparent how complain-ing, say, about a traffic jam, about politicians, about the "greedy wealthy" or the "lazy unemployed," or your col-leagues or ex-spouse, men or women, can give you a sense

of superiority. Here is why. When you complain, by implication you are right and the person or situation you complain about or react against is wrong.

There is nothing that strengthens the ego more than being
right. Being right is identification with a mental position—
a perspective, an opinion, a judgment, a story. For you to
be right, of course, you need someone else to be wrong,
and so the ego loves to make wrong in order to be right. In
other words: You need to make others wrong in order to
get a stronger sense of who you are. Not only a person, but
also a situation can be made wrong through complaining
and reactivity, which always implies that "this should not be
happening." Being right places you in a position of imagined moral superiority in relation to the person or situation
that is being judged and found wanting. It is that sense of
superiority the ego craves and through which it enhances
itself.

## IN DEFENSE OF AN ILLUSION

Facts undoubtedly exist. If you say: "Light travels faster
than sound," and someone else says the opposite is the case,
you are obviously right, and he is wrong. The simple observation that lightning precedes thunder could confirm
this. So not only are you right, but you know you are right.
Is there any ego involved in this? Possibly, but not necessarily. If you are simply stating what you know to be true,

the ego is not involved at all, because there is no identification. Identification with what? With mind and a mental position. Such identification, however, can easily creep in. If you find yourself saying, "Believe me, I know" or "Why do you never believe me?" then the ego has already crept in. It is hiding in the little word "me." A simple statement: "Light is faster than sound," although true, is now in the service of illusion, of ego. It has become contaminated with a false sense of "I"; it has become personalized, turned into a mental position. The "I" feels diminished or offended because somebody doesn't believe what "I" said.

Ego takes everything personally. Emotion arises, defensiveness, perhaps even aggression. Are you defending the truth? No, the truth, in any case, needs no defense. The light or sound does not care about what you or anybody else thinks. You are defending yourself, or rather the illusion of yourself, the mind-made substitute. It would be even more accurate to say that the illusion is defending itself. If even the simple and straightforward realm of facts can lend itself to egoic distortion and illusion, how much more so the less tangible realm of opinions, viewpoints, and judgments, all of them thought forms that can easily become infused with a sense of "I."

Every ego confuses opinions and viewpoints with facts. Furthermore, it cannot tell the difference between an event and its reaction to that event. Every ego is a master of selective perception and distorted interpretation. Only through awareness—not through thinking—can you differentiate between fact and opinion. Only through awareness are you able to see: There is the situation and here is the anger I feel about it, and then realize there are other ways of approaching the situation, other ways of seeing it and dealing with it. Only through awareness can you see the totality of the situation or person instead of adopting one limited perspective.

## TRUTH: RELATIVE OR ABSOLUTE?

Beyond the realm of simple and verifiable facts, the certainty that "I am right and you are wrong" is a dangerous thing in personal relationships as well as in interactions between nations, tribes, religions, and so on.

But if the belief "I am right; you are wrong" is one of the ways in which the ego strengthens itself, if making yourself right and others wrong is a mental dysfunction that perpetuates separation and conflict between human beings, does that mean there is no such thing as right or wrong behavior, action, or belief? And wouldn't that be the moral relativism that some contemporary Christian teachings see as the great evil of our times?

The history of Christianity is, of course, a prime example of how the belief that you are in sole possession of the truth, that is to say, right, can corrupt your actions and behavior to the point of insanity. For centuries, torturing and burning people alive if their opinion diverged even in the slightest from Church doctrine or narrow interpretations of scripture (the "Truth") was considered right because the victims were "wrong." They were so wrong that they needed to be killed. The Truth was considered more important than human life. And what was the Truth? A story you had to believe in; which means, a bundle of thoughts.

The one million people that mad dictator Pol Pot of Cambodia ordered killed included everybody who wore glasses. Why? To him, the Marxist interpretation of history was the absolute truth, and according to his version of it, those who wore glasses belonged to the educated class, the bourgeoisie, the exploiters of the peasants. They needed to be eliminated to make room for a new social order. His truth also was a bundle of thoughts.

The Catholic and other churches are actually correct when they identify relativism, the belief that there is no absolute truth to guide human behavior, as one of the evils of our times; but you won't find absolute truth if you look for it where it cannot be found: in doctrines, ideologies, sets of rules, or stories. What do all of these have in common? They are made up of thought. Thought can at best point to the truth, but it never *is* the truth. That's why Buddhists say "The finger pointing to the moon is not the moon." All religions are equally false and equally true, depending on how you use them. You can use them in the service of the ego, or you can use them in the service of the Truth. If you believe only your religion is the Truth, you are using it in the service of the ego. Used in such a way, religion becomes ideology and creates an illusory sense of superiority as well as division and conflict between people. In the service of the Truth, religious teachings represent signposts or maps left behind by awakened humans to assist you in spiritual awakening, that is to say, in becoming free of identification with form.

There is only one absolute Truth, and all other truths emanate from it. When you find that Truth, your actions will be in alignment with it. Human action can reflect the Truth, or it can reflect illusion. Can the Truth be put into words? Yes, but the words are, of course, not it. They only point to it.

The Truth is inseparable from who you are. Yes, you *are* the Truth. If you look for it elsewhere, you will be deceived every time. The very Being that you are is Truth. Jesus tried to convey that when he said, "I am the way and the truth and the life."[2] These words uttered by Jesus are one of the most powerful and direct pointers to the Truth, if understood correctly. If misinterpreted, however, they become a great obstacle. Jesus speaks of the innermost I Am, the essence identity of every man and woman, every life-form, in fact. He speaks of the life that you are. Some Christian mystics have called it the Christ within; Buddhists call it your Buddha nature; for Hindus, it is Atman, the indwelling God. When you are in touch with that dimension within yourself—and being in touch with it is your natural state, not some miraculous achievement—all your actions and relationships will reflect the oneness with all life that you sense deep within. This is love. Laws, commandments, rules, and regulations are necessary for those who are cut off from who they are, the Truth within. They prevent the worst excesses of the ego, and often they don't even do that. "Love and do what you will," said St. Augustine. Words cannot get much closer to the Truth than that.

## THE EGO IS NOT PERSONAL

On a collective level, the mind-set "We are right and they are wrong" is particularly deeply entrenched in those parts of the world where conflict between two nations, races, tribes, religions, or ideologies is long-standing, extreme, and endemic. Both sides of the conflict are equally identified with their own perspective, their own "story," that is to say, identified with thought. Both are equally incapable of seeing that another perspective, another story, may exist and also be valid. Israeli writer Y. Halevi speaks of the possibility of "accommodating a competing narrative,"[3] but in many parts of the world, people are not yet able or willing to do that. Both sides believe themselves to be in possession of the truth. Both regard themselves as victims and the "other" as evil, and because they have conceptualized and thereby dehumanized the other as the enemy, they can kill and inflict all kinds of violence on the other, even on children, without feeling their humanity and suffering. They become trapped in an insane spiral of perpetration and retribution, action and reaction.

Here it becomes obvious that the human ego in its collective aspect as "us" against "them" is even more insane than the "me," the individual ego, although the mechanism is the same. By far the greater part of violence that humans have inflicted on each other is not the work of criminals or the mentally deranged, but of normal, respectable citizens in the service of the collective ego. One can go so far as to say that on this planet "normal" equals insane. What is it that lies at the root of this insanity? Complete identification with thought and emotion, that is to say, ego.

Greed, selfishness, exploitation, cruelty, and violence are still all-pervasive on this planet. When you don't recognize them as individual and collective manifestations of an underlying dysfunction or mental illness, you fall into the error of personalizing them. You construct a conceptual identity for an individual or group, and you say: "This is who he is. This is who they are." When you confuse the ego that you perceive in others with their identity, it is the work of your own ego that uses this misperception to strengthen itself through being right and therefore superior, and through reacting with condemnation, indignation, and often anger against the perceived enemy. All this is enormously satisfying to the ego. It strengthens the sense of separation between yourself and the other, whose "otherness" has become magnified to such an extent that you can no longer feel your common humanity, nor the rootedness in the one Life that you share with each human being, your common divinity.

The particular egoic patterns that you react to most strongly in others and misperceive as their identity tend to be the same patterns that are also in you, but that you are unable or unwilling to detect within yourself. In that sense, you have much to learn from your enemies. What is it in them that you find most upsetting, most disturbing? Their selfishness? Their greed? Their need for power and control? Their insincerity, dishonesty, propensity to violence, or whatever it may be? Anything that you resent and strongly react to in another is also in you. But it is no more than a form of ego, and as such, it is completely impersonal. It has nothing to do with who that person is, nor has it anything to do with who you are. Only if you mistake it for who you are can observing it within you be threatening to your sense of self.

## WAR IS A MIND-SET

In certain cases, you may need to protect yourself or someone else from being harmed by another, but beware of making it your mission to "eradicate evil," as you are likely to turn into the very thing you are fighting against. Fighting unconsciousness will draw you into unconsciousness yourself. Unconsciousness, dysfunctional egoic behavior, can never be defeated by attacking it. Even if you defeat your opponent, the unconsciousness will simply have moved into you, or the opponent reappears in a new disguise. Whatever you fight, you strengthen, and what you resist, persists.

These days you frequently hear the expression "the war against" this or that, and whenever I hear it, I know that it is condemned to failure. There is the war against drugs, the war against crime, the war against terrorism, the war against cancer, the war against poverty, and so on. For example, despite the war against crime and drugs, there has been a dramatic increase in crime and drug-related offenses in the past twenty-five years. The prison population of the United States has gone up from just under 300,000 in 1980 to a staggering 2.1 million in 2004.[4] The war against disease has given us, amongst other things, antibiotics. At first, they were spectacularly successful, seemingly enabling us to win the war against infectious diseases. Now, many experts agree that the widespread and indiscriminate use of antibiotics has created a time bomb and that antibiotic-resistant strains of bacteria, so-called super bugs, will in all likelihood bring about a reemergence of those diseases and possibly epidemics. According to the *Journal of the American Medical Association*, medical treatment is the third-leading cause of death after heart disease and cancer in the United States. Homeopathy and Chinese medicine are two examples of possible alternative approaches to disease that do not treat the illness as an enemy and therefore do not create new diseases.

War is a mind-set, and all action that comes out of such a mind-set will either strengthen the enemy, the perceived evil, or, if the war is won, will create a new enemy, a new evil equal to and often worse than the one that was defeated. There is a deep interrelatedness between your state of consciousness and external reality. When you are in the grip of a mind-set such as "war," your perceptions become extremely selective as well as distorted. In other words, you will see only what you want to see and then misinterpret it. You can imagine what kind of action comes out of such a delusional system. Or instead of imagining it, watch the news on TV tonight.

Recognize the ego for what it is: a collective dysfunction, the insanity of the human mind. When you recognize it for what it is, you no longer misperceive it as somebody's identity. Once you see the ego for what it is, it becomes much easier to remain nonreactive toward it. You don't take it personally anymore. There is no complaining, blaming, accusing, or making wrong. Nobody is wrong. It is the ego in someone, that's all. Compassion arises when you recognize that all are suffering from the same sickness of the mind, some more acutely than others. You do not fuel the drama anymore that is part of all egoic relationships. What is its fuel? Reactivity. The ego thrives on it.

## DO YOU WANT PEACE OR DRAMA?

You want peace. There is no one who does not want peace. Yet there is something else in you that wants the drama, wants the conflict. You may not be able to feel it at this moment. You may have to wait for a situation or even just a thought that triggers a reaction in you: someone accusing you of this or that, not acknowledging you, encroaching on your territory, questioning the way you do things, an argument about money. . . . Can you then feel the enormous surge of force moving through you, the fear, perhaps being masked by anger or hostility? Can you hear your own voice becoming harsh or shrill, or louder and a few octaves lower? Can you be aware of your mind racing to defend its position, justify, attack, blame? In other words, can you awaken at that moment of unconsciousness? Can you feel that there is something in you that is at war, something that feels threatened and wants to survive at all cost, that needs the drama in order to assert its identity as the victorious character within that theatrical production? Can you feel there is something in you that would rather be right than at peace?

## BEYOND EGO: YOUR TRUE IDENTITY

When the ego is at war, know that it is no more than an illusion that is fighting to survive. That illusion thinks it is you. It is not easy at first to *be* there as the witnessing Presence, especially when the ego is in survival mode or some emotional pattern from the past has become activated, but once you have had a taste of it, you will grow in Presence power, and the ego will lose its grip on you. And so a power comes into your life that is far greater than the ego, greater than the mind. All that is required to become free of the ego is to be aware of it, since awareness and ego are incompatible. Awareness is the power that is concealed within the present moment. This is why we may also call it Presence. The ultimate purpose of human existence, which is to say, your purpose, is to bring that power into this world. And this is also why becoming free of the ego cannot be made into a goal to be attained at some point in the future. Only Presence can free you of the ego, and you can only be present Now, not yesterday or tomorrow. Only Presence can undo the past in you and thus transform your state of consciousness.

What is spiritual realization? The belief that you are spirit? No, that's a thought. A little closer to the truth than the thought that believes you are who your birth certificate says you are, but still a thought. Spiritual realization is to see clearly that what I perceive, experience, think, or feel is ultimately not who I am, that I cannot find myself in all those things that continuously pass away. The Buddha was probably the first human being to see this clearly, and so *anata* (no self) became one of the central points of his teaching. And when Jesus said, "Deny thyself," what he meant was: Negate (and thus undo) the illusion of self. If the self—ego—were truly who I am, it would be absurd to "deny" it.

What remains is the light of consciousness in which perceptions, experiences, thoughts, and feelings come and go. That is Being, that is the deeper, true I. When I know myself as that, whatever happens in my life is no longer of absolute but only of relative importance. I honor it, but it loses its absolute seriousness, its heaviness. The only thing that ultimately matters is this: Can I sense my essential Beingness, the I Am, in the background of my life at all times? To be more accurate, can I sense the I Am that I Am at this moment? Can I sense my essential identity as consciousness itself? Or am I losing myself in what happens, losing myself in the mind, in the world?

## ALL STRUCTURES ARE UNSTABLE

Whatever form it takes, the unconscious drive behind ego is to strengthen the image of who I think I am, the phantom self that came into existence when thought—a great blessing as well as a great curse—began to take over and obscured the simple yet profound joy of connectedness with Being, the Source, God. Whatever behavior the ego manifests, the hidden motivating force is always the same: the need to stand out, be special, be in control; the need for power, for attention, for more. And, of course, the need to feel a sense of separation, that is to say, the need for opposition, enemies.

The ego always wants something from other people or situations. There is always a hidden agenda, always a sense of "not enough yet," of insufficiency and lack that needs to be filled. It uses people and situations to get what it wants, and even when it succeeds, it is never satisfied for long. Often it is thwarted in its aims, and for the most part the gap between "I want" and "what is" becomes a constant source of upset and anguish. The famous and now classic pop song, "(I Can't Get No) Satisfaction," is the song of the ego. The underlying emotion that governs all the activity of the ego is fear. The fear of being nobody, the fear of nonexistence, the fear of death. All its activities are ultimately designed to eliminate this fear, but the most the ego can ever do is to cover it up temporarily with an intimate relationship, a new possession, or winning at this or that. Illusion will never satisfy you. Only the truth of who you are, if realized, will set you free.

Why fear? Because the ego arises by identification with form, and deep down it knows that no forms are permanent, that they are all fleeting. So there is always a sense of insecurity around the ego even if on the outside it appears confident.

As I was walking with a friend through a beautiful nature reserve near Malibu in California, we came upon the ruins of what had been once a country house, destroyed by a fire several decades ago. As we approached the property, long overgrown with trees and all kinds of magnificent plants, there was a sign by the side of the trail put there by the park authorities. It read: DANGER. ALL STRUCTURES ARE UNSTABLE. I said to my friend, "That's a profound sutra [sacred scripture]." And we stood there in awe. Once you realize and accept that all structures (forms) are unstable, even the seemingly solid material ones, peace arises within you. This is because the recognition of the impermanence of all forms awakens you to the dimension of the formless within yourself, that which is beyond death. Jesus called it "eternal life."

## THE EGO'S NEED TO FEEL SUPERIOR

There are many subtle but easily overlooked forms of ego that you may observe in other people and, more important, in yourself. Remember: The moment you become aware of the ego in yourself, that emerging awareness is who you are beyond ego, the deeper "I." The recognition of the false is already the arising of the real.

For example, you are about to tell someone the news of what happened. "Guess what? You don't know yet? Let me tell you." If you are alert enough, present enough, you may be able to detect a momentary sense of satisfaction within yourself just before imparting the news, even if it is bad news. It is due to the fact that for a brief moment there is, in the eyes of the ego, an imbalance in your favor between you and the other person. For that brief moment, you know *more* than the other. The satisfaction that you feel is of the ego, and it is derived from feeling a stronger sense of self relative to the other person. Even if he or she is the president or the pope, you feel superior in that moment because you know *more*. Many people are addicted to gossiping partly for this reason. In addition, gossiping often carries an element of malicious criticism and judgment of others, and so it also strengthens the ego through the implied but imagined moral superiority that is there whenever you apply a negative judgment to anyone.

If someone has more, knows more, or can do more than I, the ego feels threatened because the feeling of "less" diminishes its imagined sense of self relative to the other. It may then try to restore itself by somehow diminishing, criticizing, or belittling the value of the other person's possessions, knowledge, or abilities. Or the ego may shift its strategy, and instead of competing with the other person, it will enhance itself by association with that person, if he or she is important in the eyes of others.

## EGO AND FAME

The well-known phenomenon of "name dropping," the casual mention of who you know, is part of the ego's strategy of gaining a superior identity in the eyes of others and therefore in its own eyes through association with someone "important." The bane of being famous in this world is that who you are becomes totally obscured by a collective mental image. Most people you meet want to enhance their identity—the mental image of who they are—through association with you. They themselves may not know that they are not interested in you at all, but only in strengthening their ultimately fictitious sense of self. They believe that through you they can be more. They are looking to complete themselves through you, or rather through the mental image they have of you as a famous person, a larger-than-life collective conceptual identity.

The absurd overvaluation of fame is just one of the many manifestations of egoic madness in our world. Some famous people fall into the same error and identify with the collective fiction, the image people and the media have created of them, and they begin to actually see themselves as superior to ordinary mortals. As a result, they become more and more alienated from themselves and others, more and more unhappy, more and more dependent on their continuing popularity. Surrounded only by people who feed their inflated self-image, they become incapable of genuine relationships.

Albert Einstein, who was admired as almost superhuman and whose fate it was to become one of the most famous people on the planet, never identified with the image the collective mind had created of him. He remained humble, egoless. In fact, he spoke of "a grotesque contradiction between what people consider to be my achievements and abilities and the reality of who I am and what I am capable of."[5]

This is why it is hard for a famous person to be in a genuine relationship with others. A genuine relationship is one that is not dominated by the ego with its image-making and self-seeking. In a genuine relationship, there is an outward flow of open, alert attention toward the other person in which there is no wanting whatsoever. That alert attention is Presence. It is the prerequisite for any authentic relationship. The ego always either wants something, or if it believes there is nothing to get from the other, it is in a state of utter indifference: It doesn't care about you. And so, the three predominant states of egoic relationships are: wanting, thwarted wanting (anger, resentment, blaming, complaining), and indifference.

## CHAPTER FOUR

# Role-playing: The Many Faces of the Ego

An ego that wants something from another—and what ego doesn't—will usually play some kind of role to get its "needs" met, be they material gain, a sense of power, superiority, or specialness, or some kind of gratification, be it physical or psychological. Usually people are completely unaware of the roles they play. They *are* those roles. Some roles are subtle; others are blatantly obvious, except to the person playing it. Some roles are designed simply to get attention from others. The ego thrives on others' attention, which is after all a form of psychic energy. The ego doesn't know that the source of all energy is within you, so it seeks it outside. It is not the formless attention which is Presence that the ego seeks, but attention in some *form*, such as recognition, praise, admiration, or just to be noticed in some way, to have its existence acknowledged.

A shy person who is afraid of the attention of others is not free of ego, but has an ambivalent ego that both wants and fears attention from others. The fear is that the attention may take the form of disapproval or criticism, that is to say, something that diminishes the sense of self rather than enhances it. So the shy person's fear of attention is greater than his or her need of attention. Shyness often goes with a self-concept that is predominately negative, the belief of being inadequate. Any conceptual sense of self—seeing myself as this or that—is ego, whether predominately positive (I am the greatest) or negative (I am no good). Behind every positive self-concept is the hidden fear of not being good enough. Behind every negative self-concept is the hidden desire of being the greatest or better than others. Behind the confident ego's feeling of and continuing need for superiority is the unconscious fear of inferiority. Conversely, the shy, inadequate ego that feels inferior has a strong hidden desire for superiority. Many people fluctuate between feelings of inferiority and superiority, depending on situations or the people they come into contact with. All you need to know and observe in yourself is this: Whenever you feel superior or inferior to anyone, that's the ego in you.

## VILLAIN, VICTIM, LOVER

Some egos, if they cannot get praise or admiration, will set-
tle for other forms of attention and play roles to elicit them.
If they cannot get positive attention, they may seek negative attention instead, for example, by provoking a negative
reaction in someone else. Some children already do that
too. They misbehave to get attention. The playing of negative roles becomes particularly pronounced whenever the
ego is magnified by an active pain-body, that is to say, emotional pain from the past that wants to renew itself through
experiencing more pain. Some egos perpetrate crimes in
their search for fame. They seek attention through notori-
ety and other people's condemnation. "Please tell me that I
exist, that I am not insignificant," they seem to say. Such
pathological forms of ego are only more extreme versions
of normal egos.

Λ very common role is the one of victim, and the form
of attention it seeks is sympathy or pity or others' interest
in *my* problems, "me and my story." Seeing oneself as a victim is an element in many egoic patterns, such as complaining, being offended, outraged, and so on. Of course, once I
am identified with a story in which I assigned myself the
role of victim, I don't want it to end, and so, as every therapist knows, the ego does not want an end to its "problems"
because they are part of its identity. If no one will listen to
my sad story, I can tell it to myself in my head, over and

over, and feel sorry for myself, and so have an identity as someone who is being treated unfairly by life or other people, fate or God. It gives definition to my self-image, makes me into someone, and that is all that matters to the ego.

In the early stages of many so-called romantic relationships, role-playing is quite common in order to attract and keep whoever is perceived by the ego as the one who is going to "make me happy, make me feel special, and fulfill all my needs." "I'll play who you want me to be, and you'll play who I want you to be." That's the unspoken and unconscious agreement. However, role-playing is hard work, and so those roles cannot be sustained indefinitely, especially once you start living together. When those roles slip, what do you see? Unfortunately, in most cases, not yet the true essence of that being, but that which covers up the true essence: the raw ego divested of its roles, with its painbody, and its thwarted wanting which now turns into anger, most likely directed at the spouse or partner for having failed to remove the underlying fear and sense of lack that is an intrinsic part of the egoic sense of self.

What is commonly called "falling in love" is in most cases an intensification of egoic wanting and needing. You become addicted to another person, or rather to your image of that person. It has nothing to do with true love, which contains no wanting whatsoever. The Spanish language is the most honest in regard to conventional notions of love: *Te quiero* means "I want you" as well as "I love you." The other expression for "I love you," *te amo,* which does not have this ambiguity, is rarely used—perhaps because true love is just as rare.

## LETTING GO OF SELF-DEFINITIONS

As tribal cultures developed into the ancient civilizations, certain functions began to be allotted to certain people: ruler, priest or priestess, warrior, farmer, merchant, craftsman, laborer, and so on. A class system developed. Your function, which in most cases you were born into, determined your identity, determined who you were in the eyes of others, as well as in your own eyes. Your function became a role, but it wasn't recognized as a role: It was who you were, or thought you were. Only rare beings at the time, such as the Buddha or Jesus, saw the ultimate irrelevance of caste or social class, recognized it as identification with form and saw that such identification with the conditioned and the temporal obscured the light of the unconditioned and eternal that shines in each human being.

In our contemporary world, the social structures are less rigid, less clearly defined than they used to be. Although most people are, of course, still conditioned by their environment, they are no longer automatically assigned a function and with it an identity. In fact, in the modern world, more and more people are confused as to where they fit in, what their purpose is, and even who they are.

I usually congratulate people when they tell me, "I don't know who I am anymore." Then they look perplexed and ask, "Are you saying it is a good thing to be confused?" I ask them to investigate. What does it mean to be confused? "I don't know" is not confusion. Confusion is: "I don't know, but I should know" or "I don't know, but I need to know." Is it possible to let go of the belief that you should or need to know who you are? In other words, can you cease looking to conceptual definitions to give you a sense of self? Can you cease looking to *thought* for an identity? When you let go of the belief that you should or need to know who you are, what happens to confusion? Suddenly it is gone. When you fully accept that you don't know, you actually enter a state of peace and clarity that is closer to who you truly are than thought could ever be. Defining yourself through thought is limiting yourself.

## PRE-ESTABLISHED ROLES

Of course different people fulfill different functions in this world. It cannot be otherwise. As far as intellectual or physical abilities are concerned—knowledge, skills, talents, and energy levels—human beings differ widely. What really matters is not what function you fulfill in this world, but whether you identify with your function to such an extent that it takes you over and becomes a role that you play. When you play roles, you are unconscious. When you catch yourself playing a role, that recognition creates a space between you and the role. It is the beginning of freedom from the role. When you are completely identified with a role, you confuse a pattern of behavior with who you are, and you take yourself very seriously. You also automatically assign roles to others that correspond to yours. For example, when you visit doctors who are totally identified with their role, to them you will not be a human being but a patient or a case history.

Although the social structures in the contemporary world are less rigid than in ancient cultures, there are still many pre-established functions or roles that people readily identify with and which thus become part of the ego. This causes human interactions to become inauthentic, dehumanized, alienating. Those pre-established roles may give you a somewhat comforting sense of identity, but ultimately, you lose yourself in them. The functions people have in hierarchical organizations, such as the military, the church, a government institution, or large corporation, easily lend themselves to becoming role identities. Authentic human interactions become impossible when you lose yourself in a role.

Some pre-established roles we could call social archetypes. To mention just a few: the middle-class housewife (not as prevalent as it used to be, but still widespread); the tough macho male; the female seductress; the "nonconformist" artist or performer; a person of "culture" (a role quite common in Europe) who displays a knowledge of literature, fine art, and music in the same way as others might display an expensive dress or car. And then there is the universal role of adult. When you play that role, you take yourself and life very seriously. Spontaneity, lightheartedness, and joy are not part of that role.

The hippie movement that originated on the West Coast of the United States in the 1960s and then spread throughout the Western world came out of many young people's rejection of social archetypes, of roles, of pre-established patterns of behavior as well as egoically based social and economic structures. They refused to play the roles their parents and society wanted to impose on them. Significantly, it coincided with the horrors of the Vietnam War, in which more than 57,000 young Americans and 3 million Vietnamese died and through which the insanity of the system and the underlying mind-set was exposed for all to see. Whereas in the 1950s, most Americans were still extremely conformist in thought and behavior, in the 1960s, millions of people began to withdraw their identification with a collective conceptual identity because the insanity of the collective was so obvious. The hippie movement represented a loosening of the hitherto rigid egoic structures in the psyche of humanity. The movement itself degenerated and came to an end, but it left behind an opening, and not just in those who were part of the movement. This made it possible for ancient Eastern wisdom and spirituality to move west and play an essential part in the awakening of global consciousness.

## TEMPORARY ROLES

If you are awake enough, aware enough, to be able to observe how you interact with other people, you may detect subtle changes in your speech, attitude, and behavior depending on the person you are interacting with. At first, it may be easier to observe this in others; then, you may also detect it in yourself. The way in which you speak to the chairman of the company may be different in subtle ways from how you speak to the janitor. How you speak to a child may be different from how you speak to an adult. Why is that? You are playing roles. You are not yourself, neither with the chairman nor with the janitor or the child. When you walk into a store to buy something, when you go to a restaurant, the bank, the post office, you may find yourself slipping into pre-established social roles. You become a customer and speak and act as such. And you may be treated by the salesperson or waiter, who is also playing a role, as a customer. A range of conditioned patterns of behavior come into effect between two human beings that determine the nature of the interaction. Instead of human beings, conceptual mental images are interacting with each other. The more identified people are with their respective roles, the more inauthentic the relationships become.

You have a mental image not only of who the other person is, but also of who you are, especially in relation to the person you are interacting with. So *you* are not relating with that person at all, but who you think you are is relating to who you think the other person is and vice versa. The conceptual image your mind has made of yourself is relating to its own creation, which is the conceptual image it has made of the other person. The other person's mind has probably done the same, so every egoic interaction between two people is in reality the interaction between four conceptual mind-made identities that are ultimately fictions. It is therefore not surprising there is so much conflict in relationships. There *is* no true relationship.

## THE MONK WITH SWEATY PALMS

Kasan, a Zen teacher and monk, was to officiate at a funeral of a famous nobleman. As he stood there waiting for the governor of the province and other lords and ladies to arrive, he noticed that the palms of his hands were sweaty.

The next day he called his disciples together and confessed he was not yet ready to be a true teacher. He explained to them that he still lacked the sameness of bearing before all human beings, whether beggar or king. He was still unable to look through social roles and conceptual identities and see the sameness of being in every human. He then left and became the pupil of another master. He returned to his former disciples eight years later, enlightened.

## HAPPINESS AS A ROLE VS.
## TRUE HAPPINESS

"How are you?" "Just great. Couldn't be better." True or false?

In many cases, happiness is a role people play, and behind the smiling façade, there is a great deal of pain. Depression, breakdowns, and overreactions are common when unhappiness is covered up behind a smiling exterior and brilliant white teeth, when there is denial, sometimes even to one's self, that there is much unhappiness.

"Just fine" is a role the ego plays more commonly in America than in certain other countries where being and looking miserable is almost the norm and therefore more socially acceptable. It is probably an exaggeration, but I am told that in the capital of one Nordic country you run the risk of being arrested for drunken behavior if you smile at strangers in the street.

If there is unhappiness in you, first you need to acknowledge that it is there. But don't say, "I'm unhappy." Unhappiness has nothing to do with who you are. Say: "There is unhappiness in me." Then investigate it. A situation you find yourself in may have something to do with it.

Action may be required to change the situation or remove yourself from it. If there is nothing you can do, face what is and say, "Well, right now, this is how it is. I can either accept it, or make myself miserable." The primary cause of unhappiness is never the situation but your thoughts about it. Be aware of the thoughts you are thinking. Separate them from the situation, which is always neutral, which always is as it is. There is the situation or the fact, and here are my thoughts about it. Instead of making up stories, stay with the facts. For example, "I am ruined" is a story. It limits you and prevents you from taking effective action. "I have fifty cents left in my bank account" is a fact. Facing facts is always empowering. Be aware that what you think, to a large extent, creates the emotions that you feel. See the link between your thinking and your emotions. Rather than being your thoughts and emotions, be the awareness behind them.

Don't seek happiness. If you seek it, you won't find it, because seeking is the antithesis of happiness. Happiness is ever elusive, but freedom from unhappiness is attainable now, by facing what is rather than making up stories about it. Unhappiness covers up your natural state of well-being and inner peace, the source of true happiness.

## PARENTHOOD: ROLE OR FUNCTION?

Many adults play roles when they speak to young children. They use silly words and sounds. They talk down to the child. They don't treat the child as an equal. The fact that you temporarily know more or that you are bigger does not mean the child is not your equal. The majority of adults, at some point in their lives, find themselves being a parent, one of the most universal roles. The all-important question is: Are you able to fulfill the function of being a parent and fulfill it well, without identifying with that function, that is, without it becoming a role? Part of the necessary function of being a parent is looking after the needs of the child, preventing the child from getting into danger, and at times telling the child what to do and not to do. When being a parent becomes an identity, however, when your sense of self is entirely or largely derived from it, the function easily becomes overemphasized, exaggerated, and takes you over. Giving children what they need becomes excessive and turns into spoiling; preventing them from getting into danger becomes overprotectiveness and interferes with their need to explore the world and try things out for themselves. Telling children what to do or not to do becomes controlling, overbearing.

What is more, the role-playing identity remains in place long after the need for those particular functions has passed.

Parents then cannot let go of being a parent even when the child grows into an adult. They can't let go of the need to be needed by their child. Even when the adult child is forty years old, parents can't let go of the notion "I know what's best for you." The role of parent is still being played compulsively, and so there is no authentic relationship. Parents define themselves by that role and are unconsciously afraid of loss of identity when they cease being parents. If their desire to control or influence the actions of their adult child is thwarted—as it usually is—they will start to criticize or show their disapproval, or try to make the child feel guilty, all in an unconscious attempt to preserve their role, their identity. On the surface it looks as if they were concerned about their child, and they themselves believe it, but they are only really concerned about preserving their role-identity. All egoic motivations are self-enhancement and self-interest, sometimes cleverly disguised, even from the person in whom the ego operates.

A mother or father who identifies with the parental role may also try to become more complete through their children. The ego's need to manipulate others into filling the sense of lack it continuously feels is then directed toward them. If the mostly unconscious assumptions and motivations behind the parent's compulsion to manipulate their children were made conscious and voiced, they would probably include some or all of the following: "I want you to achieve what I never achieved; I want you to be somebody in the eyes of the world, so that I too can be some-body through you. Don't disappoint me. I sacrificed so much for you. My disapproval of you is intended to make you feel so guilty and uncomfortable that you finally con-form to my wishes. And it goes without saying that I know what's best for you. I love you and I will continue to love you if you do what I know is right for you."

When you make such unconscious motivations con-scious, you immediately see how absurd they are. The ego that lies behind them becomes visible, as does its dysfunc-tion. Some parents that I spoke to suddenly realized, "My God, is this what I have been doing?" Once you see what you are doing or have been doing, you also see its futility, and that unconscious pattern then comes to an end by it-self. Awareness is the greatest agent for change.

If your parents are doing this to you, do not tell them they are unconscious and in the grip of the ego. That will likely make them even more unconscious, because the ego will take up a defensive position. It is enough for you to recognize that it is the ego in them, that it is not who they are. Egoic patterns, even long-standing ones, sometimes dissolve almost miraculously when you don't oppose them internally. Opposition only gives them renewed strength. But even if they don't, you can then accept your parents' behavior with compassion, without needing to react to it, that is to say, without personalizing it.

Be aware also of your own unconscious assumptions or

expectations that lie behind your old, habitual reactions to them. "My parents should approve of what I do. They should understand me and accept me for who I am." Really? Why should they? The fact is they don't because they can't. Their evolving consciousness hasn't made the quantum leap to the level of awareness yet. They are not yet able to disidentify from their role. "Yes, but I can't feel happy and comfortable with who I am unless I have their approval and understanding." Really? What difference does their approval or disapproval truly make to who you are? All such unexamined assumptions cause a great deal of negative emotion, much unnecessary unhappiness.

Be alert. Are some of the thoughts that go through your mind the internalized voice of your father or mother, saying perhaps something like, "You are not good enough. You will never amount to anything," or some other judgment or mental position? If there is awareness in you, you will be able to recognize that voice in your head for what it is: an old thought, conditioned by the past. If there is awareness in you, you no longer need to believe in every thought you think. It's an old thought, no more. Awareness means Presence, and only Presence can dissolve the unconscious past in you.

"If you think you are so enlightened," Ram Dass said, "go and spend a week with your parents." That is good advice. The relationship with your parents is not only the primordial relationship that sets the tone for all subsequent relationships, it is also a good test for your degree of Presence. The more shared past there is in a relationship, the more present you need to be; otherwise, you will be forced to relive the past again and again.

## CONSCIOUS SUFFERING

If you have young children, give them help, guidance, and protection to the best of your ability, but even more important, give them space—space to be. They come into this world through you, but they are not "yours." The belief "I know what's best for you" may be true when they are very young, but the older they get, the less true it becomes. The more expectations you have of how their life should unfold, the more you are in your mind instead of being present for them. Eventually, they will make mistakes, and they will experience some form of suffering, as all humans do. In fact, they may be mistakes only from your perspective. What to you is a mistake may be exactly what your children need to do or experience. Give them as much help and guidance as you can, but realize that you may also at times have to allow them to make mistakes, especially as they begin to reach adulthood. At times, you may also have to allow them to suffer. Suffering may come to them out of the blue or it may come as the consequence of their own mistakes.

Wouldn't it be wonderful if you could spare them from

all suffering? No, it wouldn't. They would not evolve as human beings and would remain shallow, identified with the external form of things. Suffering drives you deeper. The paradox is that suffering is caused by identification with form and erodes identification with form. A lot of it is caused by the ego, although eventually suffering destroys the ego—but not until you suffer consciously.

Humanity is destined to go beyond suffering, but not in the way the ego thinks. One of the ego's many erroneous assumptions, one of its many deluded thoughts is "I should not have to suffer." Sometimes the thought gets transferred to someone close to you: "My child should not have to suffer." That thought itself lies at the root of suffering. Suffering has a noble purpose: the evolution of consciousness and the burning up of the ego. The man on the cross is an archetypal image. He is every man and every woman. As long as you resist suffering, it is a slow process because the resistance creates more ego to burn up. When you accept suffering, however, there is an acceleration of that process which is brought about by the fact that you suffer consciously. You can accept suffering for yourself, or you can accept it for someone else, such as your child or parent. In the midst of conscious suffering, there is already the transmutation. The fire of suffering becomes the light of consciousness.

The ego says, "I shouldn't have to suffer," and that

thought makes you suffer so much more. It is a distortion of the truth, which is always paradoxical. The truth is that you need to say yes to suffering before you can transcend it.

## CONSCIOUS PARENTING

Many children harbor hidden anger and resentment toward their parents and often the cause is inauthenticity in the relationship. The child has a deep longing for the parent to be there as a human being, not as a role, no matter how conscientiously that role is being played. You may be doing all the right things and the best you can for your child, but even doing the best you can is not enough. *In fact, doing is never enough if you neglect Being.* The ego knows nothing of Being but believes you will eventually be saved by doing. If you are in the grip of the ego, you believe that by doing more and more you will eventually accumulate enough "doings" to make yourself feel complete at some point in the future. You won't. You will only lose yourself in doing. The entire civilization is losing itself in doing that is not rooted in Being and thus becomes futile.

How do you bring Being into the life of a busy family, into the relationship with your child? The key is to give your child attention. There are two kinds of attention. One we might call form-based attention. The other is formless attention. Form-based attention is always connected in some way with doing or evaluating. "Have you done your homework? Eat your dinner. Tidy up your room. Brush your teeth. Do this. Stop doing that. Hurry up, get ready."

What's the next thing we have to do? This question pretty much summarizes what family life is like in many homes. Form-based attention is of course necessary and has its place, but if that's all there is in the relationship with your child, then the most vital dimension is missing and Being becomes completely obscured by doing, by "the cares of the world," as Jesus puts it. Formless attention is inseparable from the dimension of Being. How does it work?

As you look at, listen to, touch, or help your child with this or that, you are alert, still, completely present, not wanting anything other than that moment as it is. In this way, you make room for Being. In that moment, if you are present, you are not a father or mother. You are the alertness, the stillness, the Presence that is listening, looking, touching, even speaking. You are the Being behind the doing.

## RECOGNIZING YOUR CHILD

You are a human being. What does that mean? Mastery of life is not a question of control, but of finding a balance between human and Being. Mother, father, husband, wife, young, old, the roles you play, the functions you fulfill, whatever you do—all that belongs to the human dimension. It has its place and needs to be honored, but in itself it is not enough for a fulfilled, truly meaningful relationship or life. Human alone is never enough, no matter how hard you try or what you achieve. Then there is Being. It is found in the still, alert presence of Consciousness itself, the Consciousness that you are. Human is form. Being is formless. Human and Being are not separate but interwoven.

In the human dimension, you are unquestionably superior to your child. You are bigger, stronger, know more, can do more. If that dimension is all you know, you will feel superior to your child, if only unconsciously. And you will make your child feel inferior, if only unconsciously. There is no equality between you and your child because there is only form in your relationship, and in form, you are of course not equal. You may love your child, but your love will be human only, that is to say, conditional, possessive, intermittent. Only beyond form, in Being, are you equal, and only when you find the formless dimension in yourself can there be true love in that relationship. The Presence that you are, the timeless I Am, recognizes itself in another, and the other, the child in this case, feels loved, that is to say, recognized.

To love is to recognize yourself in another. The other's "otherness" then stands revealed as an illusion pertaining to the purely human realm, the realm of form. The longing for love that is in every child is the longing to be recognized, not on the level of form, but on the level of Being.

If parents honor only the human dimension of the child but neglect Being, the child will sense that the relationship is unfulfilled, that something absolutely vital is missing, and there will be a buildup of pain in the child and sometimes unconscious resentment toward the parents. "Why don't you recognize me?" This is what the pain or resentment seems to be saying.

When another recognizes you, that recognition draws the dimension of Being more fully into this world through both of you. That is the love that redeems the world. I have been speaking of this with specific reference to the relationship with your child, but it equally applies, of course, to all relationships.

It has been said "God is love" but that is not absolutely correct. God is the One Life in and beyond the countless forms of life. Love implies duality: lover and beloved, subject and object. So love is the recognition of oneness in the world of duality. This is the birth of God into the world of form. Love makes the world less worldly, less dense, more transparent to the divine dimension, the light of consciousness itself.

## GIVING UP ROLE-PLAYING

To do whatever is required of you in any situation without it becoming a role that you identify with is an essential lesson in the art of living that each one of us is here to learn.

You become most powerful in whatever you do if the action is performed for its own sake rather than as a means to protect, enhance, or conform to your role identity. Every role is a fictitious sense of self, and through it everything becomes personalized and thus corrupted and distorted by the mind-made "little me" and whatever role it happens to be playing. Most of the people who are in positions of power in this world, such as politicians, TV personalities, business as well as religious leaders, are completely identified with their role, with a few notable exceptions. They may be considered VIPs, but they are no more than unconscious players in the egoic game, a game that looks so important yet is ultimately devoid of true purpose. It is, in the words of Shakespeare, "a tale told by an idiot, full of sound and fury, signifying nothing."[1] Amazingly, Shakespeare arrived at this conclusion without having the benefit of television. If the egoic earth drama has any purpose at all, it is an indirect one: It creates more and more suffering on the planet, and suffering, although largely ego-created, is in the end also ego-destructive. It is the fire in which the ego burns itself up.

In a world of role-playing personalities, those few people who don't project a mind-made image—and there are some even on TV, in the media, and the business world—but function from the deeper core of their Being, those who do not attempt to appear more than they are but are simply themselves, stand out as remarkable and are the only ones who truly make a difference in this world. They are the bringers of the new consciousness. Whatever they do becomes empowered because it is in alignment with the purpose of the whole. Their influence, however, goes far beyond what they do, far beyond their function. Their mere presence—simple, natural, unassuming—has a transformational effect on whoever they come into contact with.

When you don't play roles, it means there is no self (ego) in what you do. There is no secondary agenda: protection or strengthening of your self. As a result, your actions have far greater power. You are totally focused on the situation. You become one with it. You don't try to be anybody in particular. You are most powerful, most effective, when you are completely yourself. But don't try to be yourself. That's another role. It's called "natural, spontaneous me." As soon as you are trying to be this or that, you are playing a role. "Just be yourself" is good advice, but it can also be misleading. The mind will come in and say, "Let's see. How can I be myself?" Then, the mind will develop some kind of strategy: "How to be myself." Another role. "How can I be myself?" is, in fact, the wrong question. It implies you have to do something to be yourself. But how doesn't apply here because you are yourself already. Just stop adding unnecessary baggage to who you already are. "But I don't know who I am. I don't know what it means to be myself." If you can be absolutely comfortable with not knowing who you are, then what's left is who you are—the Being behind the human, a field of pure potentiality rather than something that is already defined.

Give up defining yourself—to yourself or to others. You won't die. You will come to life. And don't be concerned with how others define you. When they define you, they are limiting themselves, so it's their problem. Whenever you interact with people, don't be there primarily as a function or a role, but as a field of conscious Presence.

Why does the ego play roles? Because of one unexamined assumption, one fundamental error, one unconscious thought. That thought is: I am not enough. Other unconscious thoughts follow: I need to play a role in order to get what I need to be fully myself; I need to get more so that I can be more. But you cannot be more than you are because underneath your physical and psychological form, you are one with Life itself, one with Being. In form, you are and will always be inferior to some, superior to others. In essence, you are neither inferior nor superior to anyone. True self-esteem and true humility arise out of that realization. In the eyes of the ego, self-esteem and humility are contradictory. In truth, they are one and the same.

## THE PATHOLOGICAL EGO

In a wider sense of the word, the ego itself is pathological, no matter what form it takes. When we look at the ancient Greek root of the word *pathological,* we discover just how appropriate that term is when applied to the ego. Although the word is normally used to describe a condition of disease, it is derived from *pathos,* which means suffering. This is, of course, exactly what the Buddha already discovered 2,600 years ago as a characteristic of the human condition.

A person in the grip of ego, however, does not recognize suffering as suffering, but will look upon it as the only appropriate response in any given situation. The ego in its blindness is incapable of seeing the suffering it inflicts on itself and on others. Unhappiness is an ego-created mental-emotional disease that has reached epidemic proportions. It is the inner equivalent of the environmental pollution of our planet. Negative states such as anger, anxiety, hatred, resentment, discontent, envy, jealousy, and so on, are not recognized as negative but as totally justified and are further misperceived not as self-created but as caused by someone else or some external factor. "I am holding you responsible for my pain." This is what by implication the ego is saying.

The ego cannot distinguish between a situation and its interpretation of and reaction to that situation. You might say, "What a dreadful day," without realizing that the cold, the wind, and the rain or whatever condition you react to are not dreadful. They are as they are. What is dreadful is your reaction, your inner resistance to it, and the emotion that is created by that resistance. In Shakespeare's words,

"There is nothing either good or bad, but thinking makes it so."[2] What is more, suffering or negativity is often misperceived by the ego as pleasure because up to a point the ego strengthens itself through it.

For example, anger or resentment strengthen the ego enormously by increasing the sense of separateness, emphasizing the otherness of others and creating a seemingly unassailable fortresslike mental position of "rightness." If you were able to observe the physiological changes that take place inside your body when possessed by such negative states, how they adversely affect the functioning of the heart, the digestive and immune systems, and countless other bodily functions, it would become abundantly clear that such states are indeed pathological, are forms of suffering and not pleasure.

Whenever you are in a negative state, there is something in you that wants the negativity, that perceives it as pleasurable, or that believes it will get you what you want. Otherwise, who would want to hang on to negativity, make themselves and others miserable, and create disease in the body? So, whenever there is negativity in you, if you can be aware at that moment that there is something in you that takes pleasure in it or believes it has a useful purpose, you are becoming aware of the ego directly. The moment this happens, your identity has shifted from ego to awareness. This means the ego is shrinking and awareness is growing.

If in the midst of negativity you are able to realize "At this moment I am creating suffering for myself" it will be enough to raise you above the limitations of conditioned egoic states and reactions. It will open up infinite possibilities which come to you when there is awareness—other vastly more intelligent ways of dealing with any situation. You will be free to let go of your unhappiness the moment you recognize it as unintelligent. Negativity is not intelligent. It is always of the ego. The ego may be clever, but it is not intelligent. Cleverness pursues its own little aims. Intelligence sees the larger whole in which all things are connected. Cleverness is motivated by self-interest, and it is extremely short-sighted. Most politicians and businesspeople are clever. Very few are intelligent. Whatever is attained through cleverness is short-lived and always turns out to be eventually self-defeating. Cleverness divides; intelligence includes.

## THE BACKGROUND UNHAPPINESS

The ego creates separation, and separation creates suffering. The ego is therefore clearly pathological. Apart from the obvious ones such as anger, hatred, and so on, there are other more subtle forms of negativity that are so common they are usually not recognized as such, for example, impatience, irritation, nervousness, and being "fed up." They constitute the background unhappiness that is many people's predominant inner state. You need to be extremely alert and absolutely present to be able to detect them. Whenever you do, it is a moment of awakening, of disidentification from the mind.

Here is one of the most common negative states that is easily overlooked, precisely because it is so common, so normal. You may be familiar with it. Do you often experience a feeling of discontent that could best be described as a kind of background resentment? It may be either specific or nonspecific. Many people spend a large part of their lives in that state. They are so identified with it that they cannot stand back and see it. Underlying that feeling are certain unconsciously held beliefs, that is to say, thoughts. You think these thoughts in the same way that you dream your dreams when you are asleep. In other words, you don't know you are thinking those thoughts, just as the dreamer doesn't know he is dreaming.

Here are some of the most common unconscious thoughts that feed the feeling of discontent or background resentment. I have stripped away the content from those thoughts so that the bare structure remains. They become more clearly visible that way. Whenever there is unhappiness in the background of your life (or even in the foreground), you can see which of these thoughts applies and fill in your own content according to your personal situation:

*"There is something that needs to happen in my life before I can be at peace (happy, fulfilled, etc.). And I resent that it hasn't happened yet. Maybe my resentment will finally make it happen."*

*"Something happened in the past that should not have happened, and I resent that. If that hadn't happened, I would be at peace now."*

*"Something is happening now that should not be happening, and it is preventing me from being at peace now."*

Often the unconscious beliefs are directed toward a person and so "happening" becomes "doing":

*"You should do this or that so that I can be at peace. And I resent that you haven't done it yet. Maybe my resentment will make you do it."*

*"Something you (or I) did, said, or failed to do in the past is preventing me from being at peace now."*

*"What you are doing or failing to do now is preventing me from being at peace."*

## THE SECRET OF HAPPINESS

All of the above are assumptions, unexamined thoughts that are confused with reality. They are stories the ego creates to convince you that you cannot be at peace now or cannot be fully yourself now. Being at peace and being who you are, that is, being yourself, are one. The ego says: Maybe at some point in the future, I can be at peace—if this, that, or the other happens, or I obtain this or become that. Or it says: I can never be at peace because of something that happened in the past. Listen to people's stories and they could all be entitled "Why I Cannot Be at Peace Now." The ego doesn't know that your only opportunity for being at peace *is* now. Or maybe it does know, and it is afraid that you may find this out. Peace, after all, is the end of the ego.

How to be at peace now? By making peace with the present moment. The present moment is the field on which the game of life happens. It cannot happen anywhere else. Once you have made peace with the present moment, see what happens, what you can do or choose to do, or rather what life does through you. There are three words that convey the secret of the art of living, the secret of all success and happiness: One With Life. Being one with life is being one with Now. You then realize that you don't live your life, but life lives you. Life is the dancer, and you are the dance.

The ego loves its resentment of reality. What is reality? Whatever is. Buddha called it *tatata*—the suchness of life, which is no more than the suchness of this moment. Opposition toward that suchness is one of the main features of the ego. It creates the negativity that the ego thrives on, the unhappiness that it loves. In this way, you make yourself and others suffer and don't even know that you are doing it, don't know that you are creating hell on earth. To create suffering without recognizing it—this is the essence of unconscious living; this is being totally in the grip of the ego. The extent of the ego's inability to recognize itself and see what it is doing is staggering and unbelievable. It will do exactly what it condemns others for and not see it. When it is pointed out, it will use angry denial, clever arguments, and self-justifications to distort the facts. People do it, corporations do it, governments do it. When all else fails, the ego will resort to shouting or even to physical violence. Send in the marines. We can now understand the deep wisdom in Jesus' words on the cross: "Forgive them for they know not what they do."

To end the misery that has afflicted the human condition for thousands of years, you have to start with yourself and take responsibility for your inner state at any given moment. That means now. Ask yourself, "Is there negativity in me at this moment?" Then, become alert, attentive to your thoughts as well as your emotions. Watch out for the low-level unhappiness in whatever form that I mentioned earlier, such as discontent, nervousness, being "fed up," and so on. Watch out for thoughts that appear to justify or explain this unhappiness but in reality cause it. The moment you become aware of a negative state within yourself, it does not mean you have failed. It means that you have succeeded. Until that awareness happens, there is identification with inner states, and such identification is ego. With awareness comes disidentification from thoughts, emotions, and reactions. This is not to be confused with denial. The thoughts, emotions, or reactions are recognized, and in the moment of recognizing, disidentification happens automatically. Your sense of self, of who you are, then undergoes a shift: Before you were the thoughts, emotions, and reactions; now you are the awareness, the conscious Presence that witnesses those states.

"One day I will be free of the ego." Who is talking? The ego. To become free of the ego is not really a big job but a very small one. All you need to do is be aware of your thoughts and emotions—as they happen. This is not really a "doing," but an alert "seeing." In that sense, it is true that there is nothing you can do to become free of the ego. When that shift happens, which is the shift from thinking to awareness, an intelligence far greater than the ego's cleverness begins to operate in your life. Emotions and even thoughts become depersonalized through awareness. Their impersonal nature is recognized. There is no longer a self in them. They are just human emotions, human thoughts. Your entire personal history, which is ultimately no more than a story, a bundle of thoughts and emotions, becomes of secondary importance and no longer occupies the forefront of your consciousness. It no longer forms the basis for your sense of identity. You are the light of Presence, the awareness that is prior to and deeper than any thoughts and emotions.

## PATHOLOGICAL FORMS OF EGO

As we have seen, the ego is in its essential nature pathological, if we use the word in its wider sense to denote dysfunction and suffering. Many mental disorders consist of the same egoic traits that operate in a normal person, except that they have become so pronounced that their pathological nature is now obvious to anyone, except the sufferer.

For example, many normal people tell certain kinds of lies from time to time in order to appear more important, more special, and to enhance their image in the mind of others: who they know, what their achievements, abilities, and possessions are, and whatever else the ego uses to identify with. Some people, however, driven by the ego's feeling of insufficiency and its need to have or be "more," lie habitually and compulsively. Most of what they tell you about themselves, their story, is a complete fantasy, a fictitious edifice the ego has designed for itself to feel bigger, more special. Their grandiose and inflated self-image can sometimes fool others, but usually not for long. It is then quickly recognized by most people as a complete fiction.

The mental illness that is called paranoid schizophrenia, or paranoia for short, is essentially an exaggerated form of ego. It usually consists of a fictitious story the mind has invented to make sense of a persistent underlying feeling of fear. The main element of the story is the belief that certain people (sometimes large numbers or almost everyone) are plotting against me, or are conspiring to control or kill me. The story often has an inner consistency and logic so that it sometimes fools others into believing it too. Sometimes organizations or entire nations have paranoid belief systems at their very basis. The ego's fear and distrust of other people, its tendency to emphasize the "otherness" of others by focusing on their perceived faults and make those faults into their identity, is taken a little further and makes others into inhuman monsters. The ego needs others, but its dilemma is that deep down it hates and fears them. Jean-Paul Sartre's statement "Hell is other people" is the voice of the ego. The person suffering from paranoia experiences that hell most acutely, but everyone in whom the egoic patterns still operate will feel it to some degree. The stronger the ego in you, the more likely it is that in your perception other people are the main source of problems in your life. It is also more than likely that you will make life difficult for others. But, of course, you won't be able to see that. It is always others who seem to be doing it to you.

The mental illness we call paranoia also manifests another symptom that is an element of every ego, although in paranoia it takes on a more extreme form. The more the sufferer sees himself persecuted, spied on, or threatened by others, the more pronounced becomes his sense of being the center of the universe around whom everything revolves, and the more special and important he feels as the imagined focal point of so many people's attention. His sense of being a victim, of being wronged by so many people, makes him feel very special. In the story that forms the basis of his delusional system, he often assigns to himself the role of both victim and potential hero who is going to save the world or defeat the forces of evil.

The collective ego of tribes, nations, and religious organizations also frequently contains a strong element of paranoia: us against the evil others. It is the cause of much human suffering. The Spanish Inquisition, the persecution and burning of heretics and "witches," the relations between nations leading up to the First and Second World Wars, Communism throughout its history, the "Cold War," McCarthyism in America in the 1950s, prolonged violent conflict in the Middle East are all painful episodes in human history dominated by extreme collective paranoia.

The more unconscious individuals, groups, or nations are, the more likely it is that egoic pathology will assume the form of physical violence. Violence is a primitive but still very widespread way in which the ego attempts to assert itself, to prove itself right and another wrong. With very unconscious people, arguments can easily lead to physical violence. What is an argument? Two or more people express their opinions and those opinions differ. Each person is so identified with the thoughts that make up their opinion, that those thoughts harden into mental positions which are invested with a sense of self. In other words: Identity and thought merge. Once this has happened, when I defend my opinions (thoughts), I feel and act as if I were defending my very self. Unconsciously, I feel and act as if I were fighting for survival and so my emotions will reflect this unconscious belief. They become turbulent. I am upset, angry, defensive, or aggressive. I need to win at all cost lest I become annihilated. That's the illusion. The ego doesn't know that mind and mental positions have nothing to do with who you are because the ego is the unobserved mind itself.

In Zen they say: "Don't seek the truth. Just cease to cherish opinions." What does that mean? Let go of identification with your mind. Who you are beyond the mind then emerges by itself.

## WORK—WITH AND WITHOUT EGO

Most people have moments when they are free of ego. Those who are exceptionally good at what they do may be completely or largely free of ego while performing their work. They may not know it, but their work has become a spiritual practice. Most of them are present while they do their work and fall back into relative unconsciousness in their private life. This means their state of Presence is for the time being confined to one area of their life. I have met teachers, artists, nurses, doctors, scientists, social workers, waiters, hairdressers, business owners, and salespeople who perform their work admirably without any self-seeking, fully responding to whatever the moment requires of them. They are one with what they do, one with the Now, one with the people or the task they serve. The influence such people have upon others goes far beyond the function they perform. They bring about a lessening of the ego in everyone who comes into contact with them. Even people with heavy egos sometimes begin to relax, let down their guard, and stop playing their roles when they interact with them. It comes as no surprise that those people who work without ego are extraordinarily successful at what they do. Anybody who is one with what he or she does is building the new earth.

I have also met many others who may be technically good at what they do but whose ego constantly sabotages their work. Only part of their attention is on the work they perform; the other part is on themselves. Their ego demands personal recognition and wastes energy in resentment if it doesn't get enough—and it's never enough. "Is someone else getting more recognition than me?" Or their main focus of attention is profit or power, and their work is no more than a means to that end. When work is no more than a means to an end, it cannot be of high quality. When obstacles or difficulties arise in their work, when things don't go according to expectation, when other people or circumstances are not helpful or cooperative, instead of immediately becoming one with the new situation and responding to the requirements of the present moment, they react against the situation and so separate themselves from it. There is a "me" that feels personally offended or resentful, and a huge amount of energy is burned up in useless protest or anger, energy that could be used for solving the situation if it were not being misused by the ego. What is more, this "anti"-energy creates new obstacles, new opposition. Many people are truly their own worst enemy.

People unknowingly sabotage their own work when they withhold help or information from others or try to undermine them lest they become more successful or get more credit than "me." Cooperation is alien to the ego, except when there is a secondary motive. The ego doesn't know that the more you include others, the more smoothly things flow and the more easily things come to you. When you give little or no help to others or put obstacles in their path, the universe—in the form of people and circumstances—gives little or no help to you because you have cut yourself off from the whole. The ego's unconscious core feeling of "not enough" causes it to react to someone else's success as if that success had taken something away from "me." It doesn't know that your resentment of another person's success curtails your own chances of success. In order to attract success, you need to welcome it wherever you see it.

## THE EGO IN ILLNESS

An illness can either strengthen or weaken the ego. If you complain, feel self-pity, or resent being ill, your ego becomes stronger. It also becomes stronger if you make the illness part of your conceptual identity: "I am a sufferer of such and such a disease." Ah, so now we know who you are. Some people, on the other hand, who in normal life have a big ego, suddenly become gentle and kind and much nicer people when they are ill. They may gain insights they may never have had in their normal life. They may access their inner knowing and contentment and speak words of wisdom. Then, when they get better, energy returns and so does the ego.

When you are ill, your energy level is quite low, and the intelligence of the organism may take over and use the remaining energy for the healing of the body, and so there is not enough left for the mind, that is to say, egoic thinking and emotion. The ego burns up considerable amounts of energy. In some cases, however, the ego retains the little energy that remains and uses it for its own purposes. Needless to say, those people who experience a strengthening of the ego in illness take much longer to recover. Some never do, and so the illness becomes chronic and a permanent part of their false sense of self.

## THE COLLECTIVE EGO

How hard it is to live with yourself! One of the ways in which the ego attempts to escape the unsatisfactoriness of personal selfhood is to enlarge and strengthen its sense of self by identifying with a group—a nation, political party, corporation, institution, sect, club, gang, football team.

In some cases the personal ego seems to dissolve completely as someone dedicates his or her life to working selflessly for the greater good of the collective without demanding personal rewards, recognition, or aggrandizement. What a relief to be freed of the dreadful burden of personal self. The members of the collective feel happy and fulfilled, no matter how hard they work, how many sacrifices they make. They appear to have gone beyond ego. The question is: Have they truly become free, or has the ego simply shifted from the personal to the collective?

A collective ego manifests the same characteristics as the personal ego, such as the need for conflict and enemies, the need for more, the need to be right against others who are wrong, and so on. Sooner or later, the collective will come into conflict with other collectives, because it unconsciously seeks conflict and it needs opposition to define its boundary and thus its identity. Its members will then experience the suffering that inevitably comes in the wake of any ego-motivated action. At that point, they may wake up and realize that their collective has a strong element of insanity.

It can be painful at first to suddenly wake up and realize that the collective you had identified with and worked for is actually insane. Some people at that point become cynical or bitter and henceforth deny all values, all worth. This means that they quickly adopted another belief system when the previous one was recognized as illusory and therefore collapsed. They didn't face the death of their ego but ran away and reincarnated into a new one.

A collective ego is usually more unconscious than the individuals that make up that ego. For example, crowds (which are temporary collective egoic entities) are capable of committing atrocities that the individual away from the crowd would not be. Nations not infrequently engage in behavior that would be immediately recognizable as psychopathic in an individual.

As the new consciousness emerges, some people will feel called upon to form groups that reflect the enlightened consciousness. These groups will not be collective egos. The individuals who make up these groups will have no need to define their identity through them. They no longer look to any form to define who they are. Even if the members that make up those groups are not totally free of ego yet, there will be enough awareness in them to recognize the ego in themselves or in others as soon as it appears. However, constant alertness is required since the ego *will* try to take over and reassert itself in any way it can. Dissolving the human ego by bringing it into the light of awareness—this will be one of the main purposes of these groups, whether they be enlightened businesses, charitable organizations, schools, or communities of people living together. Enlightened collectives will fulfill an important function in the arising of the new consciousness. Just as egoic collectives pull you into unconsciousness and suffering, the enlightened collective can be a vortex for consciousness that will accelerate the planetary shift.

## INCONTROVERTIBLE PROOF OF IMMORTALITY

Ego comes about through a split in the human psyche in which identity separates into two parts that we could call "I" and "me" or "me" and "myself." Every ego is therefore schizophrenic, to use the word in its popular meaning of split personality. You live with a mental image of yourself, a conceptual self that you have a relationship with. Life itself becomes conceptualized and separated from who you are when you speak of "my life." The moment you say or think "my life" and believe in what you are saying (rather than it just being a linguistic convention), you have entered the realm of delusion. If there is such a thing as "my life," it follows that I and life are two separate things, and so I can also lose my life, my imaginary treasured possession. Death becomes a seeming reality and a threat. Words and concepts split life into separate segments that have no reality in themselves. We could even say that the notion "my life" is the original delusion of separateness, the source of ego. If I and life are two, if I am separate from life, then I am separate from all things, all beings, all people. But how could I be separate from life? What "I" could there be apart from life, apart from Being? It is utterly impossible. So there is no such thing as "my life," and I don't *have* a life. I *am* life. I and life are one. It cannot be otherwise. So how could I lose my life? How can I lose something that I don't have in the first place? How can I lose something that I Am? It is impossible.

## CHAPTER FIVE

# The Pain-Body

The greater part of most people's thinking is involuntary, automatic, and repetitive. It is no more than a kind of mental static and fulfills no real purpose. Strictly speaking, you don't think: Thinking happens to you. The statement "I think" implies volition. It implies that you have a say in the matter, that there is choice involved on your part. For most people, this is not yet the case. "I think" is just as false a statement as "I digest" or "I circulate my blood." Digestion happens, circulation happens, thinking happens.

The voice in the head has a life of its own. Most people are at the mercy of that voice; they are possessed by thought, by the mind. And since the mind is conditioned by the past, you are then forced to reenact the past again and again. The Eastern term for this is karma. When you are identified with that voice, you don't know this, of course. If you knew it, you would no longer be possessed because you are only truly possessed when you mistake the possessing entity for who you are, that is to say, when you become it.

For thousands of years, humanity has been increasingly mind-possessed, failing to recognize the possessing entity as "not self." Through complete identification with the mind, a false sense of self—the ego—came into existence. The density of the ego depends on the degree to which you—the consciousness—are identified with your mind, with thinking. Thinking is no more than a tiny aspect of the totality of consciousness, the totality of who you are.

The degree of identification with the mind differs from person to person. Some people enjoy periods of freedom from it, however brief, and the peace, joy, and aliveness they experience in those moments make life worth living. These are also the moments when creativity, love, and compassion arise. Others are constantly trapped in the egoic state. They are alienated from themselves, as well as from others and the world around them. When you look at them, you may see the tension in their face, perhaps the furrowed brow, or the absent or staring expression in their eyes. Most of their attention is absorbed by thinking, and so they don't really see you, and they are not really listening to you. They are not present in any situation, their atten-

tion being either in the past or future which, of course, exist only in the mind as thought forms. Or they relate to you
through some kind of role they play and so are not themselves. Most people are alienated from who they are, and
some are alienated to such a degree that the way they behave and interact is recognized as "phony" by almost everyone, except those who are equally phony, equally alienated
from who they are.

Alienation means you don't feel at ease in any situation,
any place, or with any person, not even with yourself. You
are always trying to get "home" but never feel at home.
Some of the greatest writers of the twentieth century, such
as Franz Kafka, Albert Camus, T. S. Eliot, and James Joyce,
recognized alienation as the universal dilemma of human
existence, probably felt it deeply within themselves and so
were able to express it brilliantly in their works. They don't
offer a solution. Their contribution is to show us a reflection of the human predicament so that we can see it more
clearly. To see one's predicament clearly is a first step toward
going beyond it.

## THE BIRTH OF EMOTION

In addition to the movement of thought, although not entirely separate from it, there is another dimension to the
ego: emotion. This is not to say that all thinking and all

emotion are of the ego. They turn into ego only when you identify with them and they take you over completely, that is to say, when they become "I."

The physical organism, your body, has its own intelligence, as does the organism of every other life-form. And that intelligence reacts to what your mind is saying, reacts to your thoughts. So emotion is the body's reaction to your mind. The body's intelligence is, of course, an inseparable part of universal intelligence, one of its countless manifestations. It gives temporary cohesion to the atoms and molecules that make up your physical organism. It is the organizing principle behind the workings of all the organs of the body, the conversion of oxygen and food into energy, the heartbeat and circulation of the blood, the immune system that protects the body from invaders, the translation of sensory input into nerve impulses that are sent to the brain, decoded there, and reassembled into a coherent inner picture of outer reality. All these, as well as thousands of other simultaneously occurring functions, are coordinated perfectly by that intelligence. You don't run your body. The intelligence does. It also is in charge of the organism's responses to its environment.

This is true for any life-form. It is the same intelligence that brought the plant into physical form and then manifests as the flower that comes out of the plant, the flower that opens its petals in the morning to receive the rays of the sun and closes them at nighttime. It is the same intelligence that manifests as Gaia, the complex living being that is planet earth.

This intelligence gives rise to instinctive reactions of the organism to any threat or challenge. It produces responses in animals that appear to be akin to human emotions: anger, fear, pleasure. These instinctive responses could be considered primordial forms of emotion. In certain situations, human beings experience instinctive responses in the same way that animals do. In the face of danger, when the survival of the organism is threatened, the heart beats faster, the muscles contract, breathing becomes rapid in preparation for fight or flight. Primordial fear. When being cornered, a sudden flare-up of intense energy gives strength to the body that it didn't have before. Primordial anger. These instinctive responses appear akin to emotions, but are not emotions in the true sense of the word. The fundamental difference between an instinctive response and an emotion is this: An instinctive response is the body's direct response to some external situation. An emotion, on the other hand, is the body's response to a thought.

Indirectly, an emotion can also be a response to an actual situation or event, but it will be a response to the event seen through the filter of a mental interpretation, the filter of thought, that is to say, through the mental concepts of good and bad, like and dislike, me and mine. For example, it is likely you won't feel any emotion when you are told that someone's car has been stolen, but when it is *your* car, you will probably feel upset. It is amazing how much emotion a little mental concept like "my" can generate.

Although the body is very intelligent, it cannot tell the difference between an actual situation and a thought. It reacts to every thought as if it were a reality. It doesn't know it is just a thought. To the body, a worrisome, fearful thought means "I am in danger," and it responds accordingly, even though you may be lying in a warm and comfortable bed at night. The heart beats faster, muscles contract, breathing becomes rapid. There is a buildup of energy, but since the danger is only a mental fiction, the energy has no outlet. Part of it is fed back to the mind and generates even more anxious thought. The rest of the energy turns toxic and interferes with the harmonious functioning of the body.

## EMOTIONS AND THE EGO

The ego is not only the unobserved mind, the voice in the head which pretends to be you, but also the unobserved emotions that are the body's reaction to what the voice in the head is saying.

We have already seen what kind of thinking the egoic voice engages in most of the time and the dysfunction inherent in the structure of its thought processes, regardless of content. This dysfunctional thinking is what the body reacts to with negative emotion.

The voice in the head tells a story that the body believes in and reacts to. Those reactions are the emotions. The emotions, in turn, feed energy back to the thoughts that created the emotion in the first place. This is the vicious circle between unexamined thoughts and emotions, giving rise to emotional thinking and emotional story-making.

The emotional component of ego differs from person to person. In some egos, it is greater than in others. Thoughts that trigger emotional responses in the body may sometimes come so fast that before the mind has had time to voice them, the body has already responded with an emotion, and the emotion has turned into a reaction. Those thoughts exist at a preverbal stage and could be called unspoken, unconscious assumptions. They have their origin in a person's past conditioning, usually from early childhood. "People cannot be trusted" would be an example of such an unconscious assumption in a person whose primordial relationships, that is to say, with parents or siblings, were not supportive and did not inspire trust. Here are a few more common unconscious assumptions: "Nobody respects and appreciates me. I need to fight to survive. There is never enough money. Life always lets you down. I don't deserve abundance. I don't deserve love." Unconscious assumptions create emotions in the body which in turn generate mind activity and/or instant reactions. In this way, they create your personal reality.

The voice of the ego continuously disrupts the body's

natural state of well-being. Almost every human body is under a great deal of strain and stress, not because it is threatened by some external factor but from within the mind. The body has an ego attached to it, and it cannot but respond to all the dysfunctional thought patterns that make up the ego. Thus, a stream of negative emotion accompanies the stream of incessant and compulsive thinking.

What is a negative emotion? An emotion that is toxic to the body and interferes with its balance and harmonious functioning. Fear, anxiety, anger, bearing a grudge, sadness, hatred or intense dislike, jealousy, envy—all disrupt the energy flow through the body, affect the heart, the immune system, digestion, production of hormones, and so on. Even mainstream medicine, although it knows very little about how the ego operates yet, is beginning to recognize the connection between negative emotional states and physical disease. An emotion that does harm to the body also infects the people you come into contact with and indirectly, through a process of chain reaction, countless others you never meet. There is a generic term for all negative emotions: unhappiness.

Do positive emotions then have the opposite effect on the physical body? Do they strengthen the immune system, invigorate and heal the body? They do, indeed, but we need to differentiate between positive emotions that are ego-generated and deeper emotions that emanate from your natural state of connectedness with Being.

Positive emotions generated by the ego already contain within themselves their opposite into which they can quickly turn. Here are some examples: What the ego calls love is possessiveness and addictive clinging that can turn into hate within a second. Anticipation about an upcoming event, which is the ego's overvaluation of future, easily turns into its opposite—letdown or disappointment—when the event is over or doesn't fulfill the ego's expectations. Praise and recognition make you feel alive and happy one day; being criticized or ignored make you dejected and unhappy the next. The pleasure of a wild party turns into bleakness and a hangover the next morning. There is not good without bad, no high without low.

Ego-generated emotions are derived from the mind's identification with external factors which are, of course, all unstable and liable to change at any moment. The deeper emotions are not really emotions at all but states of Being. Emotions exist within the realm of opposites. States of Being can be obscured, but they have no opposite. They emanate from within you as the love, joy, and peace that are aspects of your true nature.

## THE DUCK WITH A HUMAN MIND

In *The Power of Now*, I mentioned my observation that after two ducks get into a fight, which never lasts long, they will separate and float off in opposite directions. Then each duck will flap its wings vigorously a few times, thus releasing the surplus energy that built up during the fight. After they flap their wings, they float on peacefully, as if nothing had ever happened.

If the duck had a human mind, it would keep the fight alive by thinking, by story-making. This would probably be the duck's story: "I don't believe what he just did. He came to within five inches of me. He thinks he owns this pond. He has no consideration for my private space. I'll never trust him again. Next time he'll try something else just to annoy me. I'm sure he's plotting something already. But I'm not going to stand for this. I'll teach him a lesson he won't forget." And on and on the mind spins its tales, still thinking and talking about it days, months, or years later. As far as the body is concerned, the fight is still continuing, and the energy it generates in response to all those thoughts is emotion, which in turn generates more thinking. This becomes the emotional thinking of the ego. You can see how problematic the duck's life would become if it had a human mind. But this is how most humans live all the time. No situation or event is ever really finished. The mind and the mind-made "me and my story" keep it going.

We are a species that has lost its way. Everything natural, every flower or tree, and every animal have important lessons to teach us if we would only stop, look, and listen. Our duck's lesson is this: Flap your wings—which translates as "let go of the story"—and return to the only place of power: the present moment.

## CARRYING THE PAST

The inability or rather unwillingness of the human mind to let go of the past is beautifully illustrated in the story of two Zen monks, Tanzan and Ekido, who were walking along a country road that had become extremely muddy after heavy rains. Near a village, they came upon a young woman who was trying to cross the road, but the mud was so deep it would have ruined the silk kimono she was wearing. Tanzan at once picked her up and carried her to the other side.

The monks walked on in silence. Five hours later, as they were approaching the lodging temple, Ekido couldn't restrain himself any longer. "Why did you carry that girl across the road?" he asked. "We monks are not supposed to do things like that."

"I put the girl down hours ago," said Tanzan. "Are you still carrying her?"

Now imagine what life would be like for someone who lived like Ekido all the time, unable or unwilling to let go internally of situations, accumulating more and more "stuff" inside, and you get a sense of what life is like for the majority of people on our planet. What a heavy burden of past they carry around with them in their minds.

The past lives in you as memories, but memories in themselves are not a problem. In fact, it is through memory that we learn from the past and from past mistakes. It is only when memories, that is to say, thoughts about the past, take you over completely that they turn into a burden, turn problematic, and become part of your sense of self. Your personality, which is conditioned by the past, then becomes your prison. Your memories are invested with a sense of self, and your story becomes who you perceive yourself to be. This "little me" is an illusion that obscures your true identity as timeless and formless Presence.

Your story, however, consists not only of mental but also of emotional memory—old emotion that is being revived continuously. As in the case of the monk who carried the burden of his resentment for five hours by feeding it with his thoughts, most people carry a large amount of unneces-sary baggage, both mental and emotional, throughout their lives. They limit themselves through grievances, regret, hostility, guilt. Their emotional thinking has become their self, and so they hang on to the old emotion because it strengthens their identity.

Because of the human tendency to perpetuate old emo-tion, almost everyone carries in his or her energy field an accumulation of old emotional pain, which I call "the pain-body."

We can, however, stop adding to the pain-body that we already have. We can learn to break the habit of accumulating and perpetuating old emotion by flapping our wings, metaphorically speaking, and refrain from mentally dwelling on the past, regardless of whether something happened yesterday or thirty years ago. We can learn not to keep situations or events alive in our minds, but to return our attention continuously to the pristine, timeless present moment rather than be caught up in mental movie-making. Our very Presence then becomes our identity, rather than our thoughts and emotions.

Nothing ever happened in the past that can prevent you from being present now; and if the past cannot prevent you from being present now, what power does it have?

## INDIVIDUAL AND COLLECTIVE

Any negative emotion that is not fully faced and seen for what it is in the moment it arises does not completely dissolve. It leaves behind a remnant of pain.

Children in particular find strong negative emotions too overwhelming to cope with and tend to try not to feel them. In the absence of a fully conscious adult who guides them with love and compassionate understanding into facing the emotion directly, choosing not to feel it is indeed the only option for the child at that time. Unfortunately, that early defense mechanism usually remains in place when the child becomes an adult. The emotion still lives in him or her unrecognized and manifests indirectly, for example, as anxiety, anger, outbursts of violence, a mood, or even as a physical illness. In some cases, it interferes with or sabotages every intimate relationship. Most psychotherapists have met patients who claimed initially to have had a totally happy childhood, and later the opposite turned out to be the case. Those may be the more extreme cases, but nobody can go through childhood without suffering emotional pain. Even if both of your parents were enlightened, you would still find yourself growing up in a largely unconscious world.

The remnants of pain left behind by every strong negative emotion that is not fully faced, accepted, and then let go of join together to form an energy field that lives in the very cells of your body. It consists not just of childhood pain, but also painful emotions that were added to it later in adolescence and during your adult life, much of it created by the voice of the ego. It is the emotional pain that is your unavoidable companion when a false sense of self is the basis of your life.

This energy field of old but still very-much-alive emotion that lives in almost every human being is the pain-body.

The pain-body, however, is not just individual in nature. It also partakes of the pain suffered by countless humans throughout the history of humanity, which is a history of continuous tribal warfare, of enslavement, pillage, rape, torture, and other forms of violence. This pain still lives in the collective psyche of humanity and is being added to on a daily basis, as you can verify when you watch the news tonight or look at the drama in people's relationships. The collective pain-body is probably encoded within every human's DNA, although we haven't discovered it there yet.

Every newborn who comes into this world already carries an emotional pain-body. In some it is heavier, more dense than in others. Some babies are quite happy most of the time. Others seem to carry an enormous amount of unhappiness within them. It is true that some babies cry a great deal because they are not given enough love and attention, but others cry for no apparent reason, almost as if they were trying to make everyone around them as unhappy as they are—and often they succeed. They have come into this world with a heavy share of human pain. Other babies may cry frequently because they can sense the emanation of their mother's and father's negative emotion, and it causes them pain and also causes their pain-body to grow already by absorbing energy from the parents' pain-bodies. Whatever the case may be, as the baby's physical body grows, so does the pain-body.

An infant with only a light pain-body is not necessarily going to be a spiritually "more advanced" man or woman than somebody with a dense one. In fact, the opposite is often the case. People with heavy pain-bodies usually have a better chance to awaken spiritually than those with a relatively light one. Whereas some of them do remain trapped in their heavy pain-bodies, many others reach a point where they cannot live with their unhappiness any longer, and so their motivation to awaken becomes strong.

Why is the suffering body of Christ, his face distorted in agony and his body bleeding from countless wounds, such a significant image in the collective consciousness of humanity? Millions of people, particularly in medieval times, would not have related to it as deeply as they did if something within themselves had not resonated with it, if they had not unconsciously recognized it as an outer representation of their own inner reality—the pain-body. They were not yet conscious enough to recognize it directly within themselves, but it was the beginning of their becoming aware of it. Christ can be seen as the archetypal human, embodying both the pain and the possibility of transcendence.

## HOW THE PAIN-BODY RENEWS ITSELF

The pain-body is a semiautonomous energy-form that lives within most human beings, an entity made up of emotion. It has its own primitive intelligence, not unlike a cunning animal, and its intelligence is directed primarily at survival. Like all life-forms, it periodically needs to feed—to take in new energy—and the food it requires to replenish itself consists of energy that is compatible with its own, which is to say, energy that vibrates at a similar frequency. Any emotionally painful experience can be used as food by the pain-body. That's why it thrives on negative thinking as well as drama in relationships. The pain-body is an addiction to unhappiness.

It may be shocking when you realize for the first time that there is something within you that periodically seeks emotional negativity, seeks unhappiness. You need even more awareness to see it in yourself than to recognize it in another person. Once the unhappiness has taken you over, not only do you not want an end to it, but you want to make others just as miserable as you are in order to feed on their negative emotional reactions.

In most people, the pain-body has a dormant and an active stage. When it is dormant, you easily forget that you carry a heavy dark cloud or a dormant volcano inside you, depending on the energy field of your particular pain-body. How long it remains dormant varies from person to person: A few weeks is the most common, but it can be a few days or months. In rare cases the pain-body can lie in hibernation for years before it gets triggered by some event.

## HOW THE PAIN-BODY FEEDS ON YOUR THOUGHTS

The pain-body awakens from its dormancy when it gets hungry, when it is time to replenish itself. Alternatively, it may get triggered by an event at any time. The pain-body that is ready to feed can use the most insignificant event as a trigger, something somebody says or does, or even a thought. If you live alone or there is nobody around at the time, the pain-body will feed on your thoughts. Suddenly, your thinking becomes deeply negative. You were most likely unaware that just prior to the influx of negative thinking a wave of emotion invaded your mind—as a dark and heavy mood, as anxiety or fiery anger. All thought is energy and the pain-body is now feeding on the energy of your thoughts. But it cannot feed on any thought. You don't need to be particularly sensitive to notice that a positive thought has a totally different feeling-tone than a negative one. It is the same energy, but it vibrates at a different frequency. A happy, positive thought is indigestible to the pain-body. It can only feed on negative thoughts because only those thoughts are compatible with its own energy field.

All things are vibrating energy fields in ceaseless motion. The chair you sit on, the book you are holding in your hands appear solid and motionless only because that is how your senses perceive their vibrational frequency, that is to say, the incessant movement of the molecules, atoms, electrons, and subatomic particles that together create what you perceive as a chair, a book, a tree, or a body. What we perceive as physical matter is energy vibrating (moving) at a particular range of frequencies. Thoughts consist of the same energy vibrating at a higher frequency than matter, which is why they cannot be seen or touched. Thoughts have their own range of frequencies, with negative thoughts at the lower end of the scale and positive thoughts at the higher. The vibrational frequency of the pain-body resonates with that of negative thoughts, which is why only those thoughts can feed the pain-body.

The usual pattern of thought creating emotion is reversed in the case of the pain-body, at least initially. Emotion from the pain-body quickly gains control of your thinking, and once your mind has been taken over by the pain-body, your thinking becomes negative. The voice in your head will be telling sad, anxious, or angry stories about yourself or your life, about other people, about past, future, or imaginary events. The voice will be blaming, accusing, complaining, imagining. And you are totally identified with whatever the voice says, believe all its distorted thoughts. At that point, the addiction to unhappiness has set in.

It is not so much that you cannot stop your train of negative thoughts, but that you don't want to. This is because the pain-body at that time is living through you, pretending to be you. And to the pain-body, pain is pleasure. It eagerly devours every negative thought. In fact, the usual voice in your head has now become the voice of the pain-body. It has taken over the internal dialogue. A vicious circle becomes established between the pain-body and your thinking. Every thought feeds the pain-body and in turn the pain-body generates more thoughts. At some point, after a few hours or even a few days, it has replenished itself and returns to its dormant stage, leaving behind a depleted organism and a body that is much more susceptible to illness. If that sounds to you like a psychic parasite, you are right. That's exactly what it is.

## HOW THE PAIN-BODY FEEDS ON DRAMA

If there are other people around, preferably your partner or a close family member, the pain-body will attempt to provoke them—push their buttons, as the expression goes—so it can feed on the ensuing drama. Pain-bodies love intimate relationships and families because that is where they get most of their food. It is hard to resist another person's pain-body that is determined to draw you into a reaction. Instinctively it knows your weakest, most vulnerable points. If it doesn't succeed the first time, it will try again and again. It is raw emotion looking for more emotion. The other person's pain-body wants to awaken yours so that both pain-bodies can mutually energize each other.

Many relationships go through violent and destructive pain-body episodes at regular intervals. It is almost unbearably painful for a young child to have to witness the emotional violence of their parents' pain-bodies, and yet that is the fate of millions of children all over the world, the nightmare of their daily existence. That is also one of the main ways in which the human pain-body is passed on from generation to generation. After each episode, the partners make up, and there is an interval of relative peace, to the limited extent that the ego allows it.

Excessive consumption of alcohol will often activate the pain-body, particularly in men, but also in some women. When a person becomes drunk, he goes through a complete personality change as the pain-body takes him over. A deeply unconscious person whose pain-body habitually replenishes itself through physical violence often directs it toward his spouse or children. When he becomes sober, he is truly sorry and may say he will never do this again, and he means it. The person who is talking and making promises, however, is not the entity that commits the violence, and so you can be sure that it will happen again and again unless he becomes present, recognizes the pain-body within himself, and thus disidentifies from it. In some cases, counseling can help him do that.

Most pain-bodies want to both inflict and suffer pain, but some are predominately either perpetrators or victims. In either case, they feed on violence, whether emotional or physical. Some couples who may think they have "fallen in love" are actually feeling drawn to each other because their respective pain-bodies complement each other. Sometimes the roles of perpetrator and victim are already clearly prescribed the first time they meet. Some marriages that are thought to be made in heaven are actually made in hell.

If you have ever lived with a cat, you will know that even when the cat seems to be asleep, it still knows what is going on, because at the slightest unusual noise, its ears will move toward it, and its eyes may open slightly. Dormant pain-bodies are the same. On some level, they are still awake, ready to jump into action when an appropriate trigger presents itself.

In intimate relationships, pain-bodies are often clever enough to lie low until you start living together and preferably have signed a contract committing yourself to be with this person for the rest of your life. You don't just marry your wife or husband, you also marry her or his pain-body—and your spouse marries yours. It can be quite a shock when, perhaps not long after moving in together or after the honeymoon, you find suddenly one day there is a complete personality change in your partner. Her voice becomes harsh or shrill as she accuses you, blames you, or shouts at you, most likely over a relatively trivial matter. Or she becomes totally withdrawn. "What's wrong?" you ask. "Nothing is wrong," she says. But the intensely hostile energy she emanates is saying, "Everything is wrong." When you look into her eyes, there is no light in them anymore; it is as if a heavy veil has descended, and the being you know and love which before was able to shine through her ego, is now totally obscured. A complete stranger seems to be looking back at you, and in her eyes there is hatred, hostility, bitterness, or anger. When she speaks to you, it is not your spouse or partner who is speaking but the pain-body speaking through them. Whatever she is saying is the pain-body's version of reality, a reality completely distorted by fear, hostility, anger, and a desire to inflict and receive more pain.

At this point you may wonder whether this is your partner's real face that you had never seen before and whether you made a dreadful mistake in choosing this person. It is, of course, not the real face, just the pain-body that temporarily has taken possession. It would be hard to find a partner who does not carry a pain-body, but it would perhaps be wise to choose someone whose pain-body is not excessively dense.

## DENSE PAIN-BODIES

Some people carry dense pain-bodies that are never completely dormant. They may be smiling and making polite conversation, but you do not need to be psychic to sense that seething ball of unhappy emotion in them just underneath the surface, waiting for the next event to react to, the next person to blame or confront, the next thing to be unhappy about. Their pain-bodies can never get enough, are always hungry. They magnify the ego's need for enemies.

Through their reactivity, relatively insignificant matters are blown up out of all proportion as they try to pull other people into their drama by getting them to react. Some get involved in protracted and ultimately pointless battles or court cases with organizations or individuals. Others are consumed by obsessive hatred toward an ex-spouse or part-ner. Unaware of the pain they carry inside, by their reac-tion, they project the pain into events and situations. Due to a complete lack of self-awareness, they cannot tell the difference between an event and their reaction to the event. To them, the unhappiness and even the pain itself is out there in the event or situation. Being unconscious of their inner state, they don't even know that they are deeply un-happy, that they are suffering.

Sometimes people with such dense pain-bodies become activists fighting for a cause. The cause may indeed be wor-thy, and they are sometimes successful at first in getting things done; however, the negative energy that flows into what they say and do and their unconscious need for ene-mies and conflict tend to generate increasing opposition to their cause. Usually they also end up creating enemies within their own organization, because wherever they go, they find reasons for feeling bad, and so their pain-body continues to find exactly what it is looking for.

## ENTERTAINMENT, THE MEDIA, AND THE PAIN-BODY

If you were not familiar with our contemporary civiliza-tion, if you had come here from another age or another planet, one of the things that would amaze you is that millions of people love and pay money to watch humans kill and inflict pain on each other and call it "entertainment."

Why do violent films attract such large audiences? There is an entire industry, a large part of which fuels the human addiction to unhappiness. People obviously watch those films because they want to feel bad. What is it in humans that loves to feel bad and calls it good? The pain-body, of course. A large part of the entertainment industry caters to it. So, in addition to reactivity, negative thinking, and personal drama, the pain-body also renews itself vicariously through the cinema and television screen. Pain-bodies write and produce these films, and pain-bodies pay to watch them.

Is it always "wrong" to show and watch violence on television and the cinema screen? Does all such violence cater to the pain-body? At the current evolutionary stage of humanity, violence is still not only all-pervasive but even on the increase, as the old egoic consciousness, amplified by the collective pain-body, intensifies prior to its inevitable demise. If films show violence in its wider context, if they show its origin and its consequences, show what it does to the victim as well as the perpetrator, show the collective unconsciousness that lies behind it and is passed on from generation to generation (the anger and hatred that lives in humans as the pain-body), then those films can fulfill a vital function in the awakening of humanity. They can act as a mirror in which humanity sees its own insanity. That in you which recognizes madness as madness (even if it is your own) is sanity, is the arising awareness, is the end of insanity.

Such films do exist and they do not fuel the pain-body. Some of the best antiwar films are films that show the reality of war rather than a glamorized version of it. The pain-body can only feed on films in which violence is portrayed as normal or even desirable human behavior, or that glorify violence with the sole purpose of generating negative emotion in the viewer and so become a "fix" for the pain-addicted pain-body.

The popular tabloid press does not primarily sell news but negative emotion—food for the pain-body. "Outrage" screams the three-inch headline, or "Bastards." The British tabloid press excels at this. They know that negative emotion sells far more papers than news does.

There is a tendency in the news media in general, including television, to thrive on negative news. The worse things get, the more excited the presenters become, and often the negative excitement is generated by the media itself. Pain-bodies just love it.

## THE COLLECTIVE FEMALE PAIN-BODY

The collective dimension of the pain-body has different strands in it. Tribes, nations, races, all have their own collective pain-body, some heavier than others, and most members of that tribe, nation, or race have a share in it to a greater or lesser degree.

Almost every woman has her share in the collective female pain-body, which tends to become activated particularly just prior to the time of menstruation. At that time many women become overwhelmed by intense negative emotion.

The suppression of the feminine principle especially over the past two thousand years has enabled the ego to gain absolute supremacy in the collective human psyche. Although women have egos, of course, the ego can take root and grow more easily in the male form than in the female. This is because women are less mind-identified than men. They are more in touch with the inner body and the intelligence of the organism where the intuitive faculties originate. The female form is less rigidly encapsulated than the male, has greater openness and sensitivity toward other life-forms, and is more attuned to the natural world.

If the balance between male and female energies had not been destroyed on our planet, the ego's growth would have been greatly curtailed. We would not have declared war on nature, and we would not be so completely alienated from our Being.

Nobody knows the exact figure because records were not kept, but it seems certain that during a three-hundred-year period between three and five million women were tortured and killed by the "Holy Inquisition," an institution founded by the Roman Catholic Church to suppress heresy. This surely ranks together with the Holocaust as one of the darkest chapters in human history. It was enough for a woman to show a love for animals, walk alone in the fields or woods, or gather medicinal plants to be branded a witch, then tortured and burned at the stake. The sacred feminine was declared demonic, and an entire dimension largely disappeared from human experience. Other cultures and religions, such as Judaism, Islam, and even Buddhism, also suppressed the female dimension, although in a less violent way. Women's status was reduced to being child bearers and men's property. Males who denied the feminine even within themselves were now running the world, a world that was totally out of balance. The rest is history or rather a case history of insanity.

Who was responsible for this fear of the feminine that could only be described as acute collective paranoia? We could say: Of course, men were responsible. But then why in many ancient pre-Christian civilizations such as the Sumerian, Egyptian, and Celtic were women respected and the feminine principle not feared but revered? What is it that suddenly made men feel threatened by the female? The evolving ego in them. It knew it could gain full control of our planet only through the male form, and to do so, it had to render the female powerless.

In time, the ego also took over most women, although it could never become as deeply entrenched in them as in men.

We now have a situation in which the suppression of the feminine has become internalized, even in most women. The sacred feminine, because it is suppressed, is felt by many women as emotional pain. In fact, it has become part of their pain-body, together with the accumulated pain suffered by women over millennia through childbirth, rape, slavery, torture, and violent death.

But things are changing rapidly now. With many people becoming more conscious, the ego is losing its hold on the human mind. Because the ego was never as deeply rooted in woman, it is losing its hold on women more quickly than on men.

## NATIONAL AND RACIAL PAIN-BODIES

Certain countries in which many acts of collective violence were suffered or perpetrated have a heavier collective pain-body than others. This is why older nations tend to have stronger pain-bodies. It is also why younger countries, such as Canada or Australia, and those that have remained more sheltered from the surrounding madness, such as Switzerland, tend to have lighter collective pain-bodies. Of course, in those countries, people still have their personal pain-body to deal with. If you are sensitive enough, you can feel a heaviness in the energy field of certain countries as soon as you step off the plane. In other countries, one can sense an energy field of latent violence just underneath the surface of everyday life. In some nations, for example, in the Middle East, the collective pain-body is so acute that a significant part of the population finds itself forced to act it out in an endless and insane cycle of perpetration and retribution through which the pain-body renews itself continuously.

In countries where the pain-body is heavy but no longer acute, there has been a tendency for people to try and desensitize themselves to the collective emotional pain: in Germany and Japan through work, in some other countries through widespread indulgence in alcohol (which, however, can also have the opposite effect of stimulating the pain-body, particularly if consumed in excess). China's heavy pain-body is to some extent mitigated by the widespread practice of t'ai chi, which amazingly was not declared illegal by the Communist government that otherwise feels threatened by anything it cannot control. Every day in the streets and city parks, millions practice this movement meditation that stills the mind. This makes a considerable difference to the collective energy field and goes some way toward diminishing the pain-body by reducing thinking and generating Presence.

Spiritual practices that involve the physical body, such as

t'ai chi, qigong, and yoga, are also increasingly being embraced in the Western world. These practices do not create a separation between body and spirit and are helpful in weakening the pain-body. They will play an important role in the global awakening.

The collective racial pain-body is pronounced in Jewish people, who have suffered persecution over many centuries. Not surprisingly, it is strong as well in Native Americans, whose numbers were decimated and whose culture all but destroyed by the European settlers. In Black Americans too the collective pain-body is pronounced. Their ancestors were violently uprooted, beaten into submission, and sold into slavery. The foundation of American economic prosperity rested on the labor of four to five million black slaves. In fact, the suffering inflicted on Native and Black Americans has not remained confined to those two races, but has become part of the collective American pain-body. It is always the case that both victim and perpetrator suffer the consequences of any acts of violence, oppression, or brutality. For what you do to others, you do to yourself.

It doesn't really matter what proportion of your pain-body belongs to your nation or race and what proportion is personal. In either case, you can only go beyond it by taking responsibility for your inner state now. Even if blame seems more than justified, as long as you blame others, you keep feeding the pain-body with your thoughts and remain trapped in your ego. There is only one perpetrator of evil on the planet: human unconsciousness. That realization is true forgiveness. With forgiveness, your victim identity dissolves, and your true power emerges—the power of Presence. Instead of blaming the darkness, you bring in the light.

## CHAPTER SIX

# Breaking Free

The beginning of freedom from the pain-body lies first of all in the realization that you *have* a pain-body. Then, more important, in your ability to stay present enough, alert enough, to notice the pain-body in yourself as a heavy influx of negative emotion when it becomes active. When it is recognized, it can no longer pretend to be you and live and renew itself through you.

It is your conscious Presence that breaks the identification with the pain-body. When you don't identify with it, the pain-body can no longer control your thinking and so cannot renew itself anymore by feeding on your thoughts. The pain-body in most cases does not dissolve immediately, but once you have severed the link between it and your thinking, the pain-body begins to lose energy. Your thinking ceases to be clouded by emotion; your present perceptions are no longer distorted by the past. The energy that was trapped in the pain-body then changes its vibrational frequency and is transmuted into Presence. In this way, the pain-body becomes fuel for consciousness. This is why many of the wisest, most enlightened men and women on our planet once had a heavy pain-body.

Regardless of what you say or do or what face you show to the world, your mental-emotional state cannot be concealed. Every human being emanates an energy field that corresponds to his or her inner state, and most people can sense it, although they may feel someone else's energy emanation only subliminally. That is to say, they don't know that they sense it, yet it determines to a large extent how they feel about and react to that person. Some people are most clearly aware of it when they first meet someone, even before any words are exchanged. A little later, however, words take over the relationship and with words come the roles that most people play. Attention then moves to the realm of mind, and the ability to sense the other person's energy field becomes greatly diminished. Nevertheless, it is still felt on an unconscious level.

When you realize that pain-bodies unconsciously seek more pain, that is to say, that they want something bad to happen, you will understand that many traffic accidents are caused by drivers whose pain-bodies are active at the time.

When two drivers with active pain-bodies arrive at an intersection at the same time, the likelihood of an accident is many times greater than under normal circumstances. Unconsciously they both want the accident to happen. The role of pain-bodies in traffic accidents is most obvious in the phenomenon called "road rage," when drivers become physically violent often over a trivial matter such as someone in front of them driving too slowly.

Many acts of violence are committed by "normal" people who temporarily turn into maniacs. All over the world at court proceedings you hear the defense lawyers say, "This is totally out of character," and the accused, "I don't know what came over me." To my knowledge so far, no defense lawyer has said to the judge—although the day may not be far off—"This is a case of diminished responsibility. My client's pain-body was activated, and he did not know what he was doing. In fact, he didn't do it. His pain-body did."

Does this mean that people are not responsible for what they do when possessed by the pain-body? My answer is: How can they be? How can you be responsible when you are unconscious, when you don't know what you are doing? However, in the greater scheme of things, human beings are meant to evolve into conscious beings, and those who don't will suffer the consequences of their unconsciousness. They are out of alignment with the evolutionary impulse of the universe.

And even that is only relatively true. From a higher

perspective, it is not possible to be out of alignment with the evolution of the universe, and even human unconsciousness and the suffering it generates is part of that evolution. When you can't stand the endless cycle of suffering anymore, you begin to awaken. So the pain-body too has its necessary place in the larger picture.

## PRESENCE

A woman in her thirties came to see me. As she greeted me, I could sense the pain behind her polite and superficial smile. She started telling me her story, and within one second her smile changed into a grimace of pain. Then, she began to sob uncontrollably. She said she felt lonely and unfulfilled. There was much anger and sadness. As a child she had been abused by a physically violent father. I saw quickly that her pain was not caused by her present life circumstances but by an extraordinarily heavy pain-body. Her pain-body had become the filter through which she viewed her life situation. She was not yet able to see the link between the emotional pain and her thoughts, being completely identified with both. She could not yet see that she was feeding the pain-body with her thoughts. In other words, she lived with the burden of a deeply unhappy self. At some level, however, she must have realized that her pain originated within herself, that she was a burden to herself. She was ready to awaken, and this is why she had come.

I directed the focus of her attention to what she was feeling inside her body and asked her to sense the emotion directly, instead of through the filter of her unhappy thoughts, her unhappy story. She said she had come expecting me to show her the way out of her unhappiness, not into it. Reluctantly, however, she did what I asked her to do. Tears were rolling down her face, her whole body was shaking. "At this moment, this is what you feel," I said. "There is nothing you can do about the fact that *at this moment* this is what you feel. Now, instead of wanting this moment to be different from the way it is, which adds more pain to the pain that is already there, is it possible for you to completely accept that this is what you feel right now?"

She was quiet for a moment. Suddenly she looked impatient, as if she was about to get up, and said angrily, "No, I don't want to accept this." "Who is speaking?" I asked her. "You or the unhappiness in you? Can you see that your unhappiness about being unhappy is just another layer of unhappiness?" She became quiet again. "I am not asking you to *do* anything. All I'm asking is that you find out whether it is possible for you to allow those feelings to be there. In other words, and this may sound strange, if you don't mind being unhappy, what happens to the unhappiness? Don't you want to find out?"

She looked puzzled briefly, and after a minute or so of sitting silently, I suddenly noticed a significant shift in her energy field. She said, "This is weird. I'm still unhappy, but now there is space around it. It seems to matter less." This was the first time I heard somebody put it like that: There is space around my unhappiness. That space, of course, comes when there is inner acceptance of whatever you are experiencing in the present moment.

I didn't say much else, allowing her to be with the experience. Later she came to understand that the moment she stopped identifying with the feeling, the old painful emotion that lived in her, the moment she put her attention on it directly without trying to resist it, it could no longer control her thinking and so become mixed up with a mentally constructed story called "The Unhappy Me." Another dimension had come into her life that transcended her personal past—the dimension of Presence. Since you cannot be unhappy without an unhappy story, this was the end of her unhappiness. It was also the beginning of the end of her pain-body. Emotion in itself is not unhappiness. Only emotion plus an unhappy story is unhappiness.

When our session came to an end, it was fulfilling to know that I had just witnessed the arising of Presence in another human being. The very reason for our existence in human form is to bring that dimension of consciousness into this world. I had also witnessed a diminishment of the pain-body, not through fighting it but through bringing the light of consciousness to it.

A few minutes after my visitor left, a friend arrived to drop something off. As soon as she came into the room she said, "What happened here? The energy feels heavy and murky. It almost makes me feel sick. You need to open the windows, burn some incense." I explained that I had just witnessed a major release in someone with a very dense pain-body and that what she felt must be some of the energy that was released during our session. My friend, however, didn't want to stay and listen. She wanted to get away as soon as possible.

I opened the windows and went out to have dinner at a small Indian restaurant nearby. What happened there was a clear, further confirmation of what I already knew: That on some level, all seemingly individual human pain-bodies are connected. Although the form this particular confirmation took did come as a shock.

## THE RETURN OF THE PAIN-BODY

I sat down at a table and ordered a meal. There were a few other guests. At a nearby table, there was a middle-aged man in a wheelchair who was just finishing his meal. He glanced at me once, briefly but intensely. A few minutes passed. Suddenly he became restless, agitated, his body began twitching. The waiter came to take his plate. The man started arguing with him. "The food was no good. It was dreadful." "Then why did you eat it?" asked the waiter. And that really set him off. He started shouting, became abusive. Vile words were coming out of his mouth; intense, violent hatred filled the room. One could feel that energy entering the cells of one's body looking for something to latch on to. Now he was shouting at the other guests too, but for some strange reason ignoring me completely as I sat in intense Presence. I suspected that the universal human pain-body had come back to tell me, "You thought you defeated me. Look, I'm still here." I also considered the possibility that the released energy field left behind after our session followed me to the restaurant and attached itself to the one person in whom it found a compatible vibrational frequency, that is to say, a heavy pain-body.

The manager opened the door, "Just leave. Just leave." The man zoomed out in his electric wheelchair, leaving everyone stunned. One minute later he returned. His pain-body wasn't finished yet. It needed more. He pushed open the door with his wheelchair, shouting obscenities. A waitress tried to stop him from coming in. He put his chair in fast-forward and pinned her against the wall. Other guests jumped up and tried to pull him away. Shouting, screaming, pandemonium. A little later a policeman arrived, the man became quiet, was asked to leave and not return. The waitress fortunately was not hurt, except for bruises on her legs. When it was all over, the manager came to my table and asked me, half joking but perhaps feeling intuitively that there was some connection, "Did you cause all this?"

## THE PAIN-BODY IN CHILDREN

Children's pain-bodies sometimes manifest as moodiness or withdrawal. The child becomes sullen, refuses to interact, and may sit in a corner, hugging a doll or sucking a thumb. They can also manifest as weeping fits or temper tantrums. The child screams, may throw him or herself on the floor, or become destructive. Thwarted wanting can easily trigger the pain-body, and in a developing ego, the force of wanting can be intense. Parents may watch helplessly in incomprehension and disbelief as their little angel becomes transformed within a few seconds into a little monster. "Where does all that unhappiness come from?" they wonder. To a greater or lesser extent, it is the child's share of the collective pain-body of humanity which goes back to the very origin of the human ego.

But the child may also already have taken on pain from his or her parents' pain-bodies, and so the parents may see in the child a reflection of what is also in them. Highly sensitive children are particularly affected by their parents' pain-bodies. Having to witness their parents' insane drama causes almost unbearable emotional pain, and so it is often these sensitive children who grow into adults with heavy pain-bodies. Children are not fooled by parents who try to hide their pain-body from them, who say to each other, "We mustn't fight in front of the children." This usually means while the parents make polite conversation, the home is pervaded with negative energy. Suppressed pain-bodies are extremely toxic, even more so than openly active ones, and that psychic toxicity is absorbed by the children and contributes to the development of their own pain-body.

Some children learn subliminally about ego and pain-body simply by living with very unconscious parents. A woman whose parents both had strong egos and heavy pain-bodies told me that often when her parents were shouting and screaming at each other, she would look at them and although she loved them, would say to herself, "These people are nuts. How did I ever end up here?" There was already an awareness in her of the insanity of living in such a way. That awareness helped reduce the amount of pain she absorbed from her parents.

Parents often wonder how to deal with their child's pain-body. The primary question is, of course, are they dealing with their own? Do they recognize it within themselves? Are they able to stay present enough when it becomes activated so that they can be aware of the emotion on the feeling level before it gets a chance to turn into thinking and thus into an "unhappy person"?

While the child is having a pain-body attack, there isn't much you can do except to stay present so that you are not drawn into an emotional reaction. The child's pain-body would only feed on it. Pain-bodies can be extremely dramatic. Don't buy into the drama. Don't take it too seriously. If the pain-body was triggered by thwarted wanting, don't give in now to its demands. Otherwise, the child will learn: "The more unhappy I become, the more likely I am to get what I want." This is a recipe for dysfunction in later life. The pain-body will be frustrated by your nonreaction and may briefly act up even more before it subsides. Fortunately, pain-body episodes in children are usually more short-lived than in adults.

A little while after it has subsided, or perhaps the next day, you can talk to the child about what happened. But don't *tell* the child about the pain-body. Ask questions instead. For example: "What was it that came over you yesterday when you wouldn't stop screaming? Do you remember? What did it feel like? Was it a good feeling? That thing that came over you, does it have a name? No? If it had a name, what would it be called? If you could see it, what would it look like? Can you paint a picture of what it would look like? What happened to it when it went away? Did it go to sleep? Do you think it may come back?"

These are just a few suggested questions. All these questions are designed to awaken the witnessing faculty in the child, which is Presence. They will help the child to disidentify from the pain-body. You may also want to talk to the child about your own pain-body using the child's terminology. The next time the child gets taken over by the pain-body, you can say, "It's come back, hasn't it?" Use whatever words the child used when you talked about it. Direct the child's attention to what it *feels* like. Let your attitude be one of interest or curiosity rather than one of criticism or condemnation.

It is unlikely that this will stop the pain-body in its tracks, and it may appear that the child will not even be hearing you, yet some awareness will remain in the background of the child's consciousness even while the pain-body is active. After a few times, the awareness will have grown stronger and the pain-body will have weakened. The child is growing in Presence. One day you may find that the child is the one to point out to you that your own pain-body has taken control of you.

## UNHAPPINESS

Not all unhappiness is of the pain-body. Some of it is new unhappiness, created whenever you are out of alignment with the present moment, when the Now is denied in one way or another. When you recognize that the present moment is always already the case and therefore inevitable, you can bring an uncompromising inner "yes" to it and so not only create no further unhappiness, but, with inner resistance gone, find yourself empowered by Life itself.

The pain-body's unhappiness is always clearly out of proportion to the apparent cause. In other words, it is an overreaction. This is how it is recognized, although not usually by the sufferer, the person possessed. Someone with a heavy pain-body easily finds reasons for being upset, angry, hurt, sad, or fearful. Relatively insignificant things that someone else would shrug off with a smile or not even notice become the apparent cause of intense unhappiness. They are, of course, not the true cause but only act as a trigger. They bring back to life the old accumulated emotion. The emotion then moves into the head and amplifies and energizes the egoic mind structures.

Pain-body and ego are close relatives. They need each other. The triggering event or situation is then interpreted and reacted to through the screen of a heavily emotional ego. This is to say, its significance becomes completely distorted. You look at the present through the eyes of the emotional past within you. In other words, what you see and experience is not in the event or situation but in you. Or in some cases, it may be there in the event or situation, but you amplify it through your reaction. This reaction, this amplification, is what the pain-body wants and needs, what it feeds on.

For someone possessed by a heavy pain-body, it is often impossible to step outside his or her distorted interpretation, the heavily emotional "story." The more negative emotion there is in a story, the heavier and more impenetrable it becomes. And so the story is not recognized as such but is taken to be reality. When you are completely trapped in the movement of thought and the accompanying emotion, stepping outside is not possible because you don't even know that there is an outside. You are trapped in your own

movie or dream, trapped in your own hell. To you it is
reality and no other reality is possible. And as far as you are
concerned, your reaction is the only possible reaction.

## BREAKING IDENTIFICATION
## WITH THE PAIN-BODY

A person with a strong, active pain-body has a particular
energy emanation that other people perceive as extremely
unpleasant. When they meet such a person, some people
will immediately want to remove themselves or reduce interaction with him or her to a minimum. They feel re-
pulsed by the person's energy field. Others will feel a wave
of aggression toward this person, and they will be rude or
attack him or her verbally and in some cases, even physically. This means there is something within them that resonates with the other person's pain-body. What they react
to so strongly is also in them. It is their own pain-body.

Not surprisingly, people with heavy and frequently active pain-bodies often find themselves in conflict situations.
Sometimes, of course, they actively provoke them. But at
other times, they may not actually do anything. The negativity they emanate is enough to attract hostility and generate conflict. It requires a high degree of Presence to avoid
reacting when confronted by someone with such an active
pain-body. If you are able to stay present, it sometimes happens that your Presence enables the other person to dis-

identify from his or her own pain-body and thus experience the miracle of a sudden awakening. Although the awakening may be short-lived, the awakening process will have become initiated.

One of the first such awakenings that I witnessed happened many years ago. My doorbell rang close to eleven o'clock at night. My neighbor Ethel's anxiety-laden voice came through the intercom. "We need to talk. This is very important. Please let me in." Ethel was middle-aged, intelligent, and highly educated. She also had a strong ego and a heavy pain-body. She escaped from Nazi Germany when she was an adolescent, and many of her family members perished in the concentration camps.

Ethel sat down on my sofa, agitated, her hands trembling. She took letters and documents out of the file she carried with her and spread them out all over the sofa and floor. At once I had the strange sensation as if a dimmer switch had turned the inside of my entire body to maximum power. There was nothing to do other than remain open, alert, intensely present—present with every cell of the body. I looked at her with no thought and no judgment and listened in stillness without any mental commentary. A torrent of words came out of her mouth. "They sent me another disturbing letter today. They are conducting a vendetta against me. You must help. We need to fight them together. Their crooked lawyers will stop at nothing. I will lose my home. They are threatening me with dispossession."

It transpired that she refused to pay the service charge because the property managers had failed to carry out some repairs. They in turn threatened to take her to court.

She talked for ten minutes or so. I sat, looked, and listened. Suddenly she stopped talking, looked at the papers all around her as if she had just woken up from a dream. She became calm and gentle. Her entire energy field changed. Then she looked at me and said, "This isn't important at all, is it?" "No, it isn't," I said. She sat quietly for a couple more minutes, then picked up her papers and left. The next morning she stopped me in the street, looking at me somewhat suspiciously. "What did you do to me? Last night was the first night in years that I slept well. In fact, I slept like a baby."

She believed I had "done something" to her, but I had done nothing. Instead of asking what I had done to her, perhaps she should have asked what I had not done. I had not reacted, not confirmed the reality of her story, not fed her mind with more thought and her pain-body with more emotion. I had allowed her to experience whatever she was experiencing at that moment, and the power of allowing lies in noninterference, nondoing. Being present is always infinitely more powerful than anything one could say or do, although sometimes being present can give rise to words or actions.

What happened to her was not yet a permanent shift, but a glimpse of what is possible, a glimpse of what was already within her. In Zen, such a glimpse is called *satori*. Satori is a moment of Presence, a brief stepping out of the voice in your head, the thought processes, and their reflection in the body as emotion. It is the arising of inner spaciousness where before there was the clutter of thought and the turmoil of emotion.

The thinking mind cannot understand Presence and so will often misinterpret it. It will say that you are uncaring, distant, have no compassion, are not relating. The truth is, you are relating but at a level deeper than thought and emotion. In fact, at that level there is a true coming together, a true joining that goes far beyond relating. In the stillness of Presence, you can sense the formless essence in yourself and in the other as one. Knowing the oneness of yourself and the other is true love, true care, true compassion.

## "TRIGGERS"

Some pain-bodies react to only one particular kind of trigger or situation, which is usually one that resonates with a certain kind of emotional pain suffered in the past. For example, if a child grows up with parents for whom financial issues are the source of frequent drama and conflict, he or she may absorb the parents' fear around money and develop a pain-body that is triggered whenever financial issues are involved. The child as adult gets upset or angry even over insignificant amounts of money. Behind the upset or anger lies issues of survival and intense fear. I have seen spiritual, that is to say, relatively conscious, people who started to shout, blame, and make accusations the moment they picked up the phone to talk to their stockbroker or realtor. Just as there is a health warning on every package of cigarettes, perhaps there should be similar warnings on every banknote and bank statement: "Money can activate the pain-body and cause complete unconsciousness."

Someone who in childhood was neglected or abandoned by one or both parents will likely develop a pain-body that becomes triggered in any situation that resonates even remotely with their primordial pain of abandonment. A friend arriving a few minutes late to pick them up at the airport or a spouse coming home late can trigger a major pain-body attack. If their partner or spouse leaves them or dies, the emotional pain they experience goes far beyond the pain that is natural in such a situation. It may be intense anguish, long-lasting, incapacitating depression, or obsessive anger.

A woman who in childhood was physically abused by her father may find that her pain-body becomes easily activated in any close relationship with a man. Alternatively, the emotion that makes up her pain-body may draw her to a man whose pain-body is similar to that of her father. Her pain-body may feel a magnetic pull to someone who it senses will give it more of the same pain. That pain is sometimes misinterpreted as falling in love.

178

A man who had been an unwanted child and was given no love and a minimum of care and attention by his mother developed a heavy ambivalent pain-body that consisted of unfulfilled intense longing for his mother's love and attention and at the same time intense hatred toward her for withholding what he so desperately needed. When he became an adult, almost every woman would trigger his pain-body's neediness—a form of emotional pain—and this would manifest as an addictive compulsion to "conquer and seduce" almost every woman he met and in this way get the female love and attention that the pain-body craved. He became quite an expert on seduction, but as soon as a relationship turned intimate or his advances were rejected, the pain-body's anger toward his mother would come up and sabotage the relationship.

When you recognize your own pain-body as it arises, you will also quickly learn what the most common triggers are that activate it, whether it be situations or certain things other people do or say. When those triggers occur, you will immediately see them for what they are and enter a heightened state of alertness. Within a second or two, you will also notice the emotional reaction that is the arising pain-body, but in that state of alert Presence, you won't identify with it, which means the pain-body cannot take you over and become the voice in your head. If you are with your partner at the time, you may tell him or her: "What you just said (or did) triggered my pain-body." Have an agreement with your partner that whenever either of you says or does something that triggers the other person's pain-body, you will immediately mention it. In this way, the pain-body can no longer renew itself through drama in the relationship and instead of pulling you into unconsciousness, will help you become fully present.

Every time you are present when the pain-body arises, some of the pain-body's negative emotional energy will burn up, as it were, and become transmuted into Presence. The rest of the pain-body will quickly withdraw and wait for a better opportunity to arise again, that is to say, when you are less conscious. A better opportunity for the pain-body to arise may come whenever you lose Presence, perhaps after you have had a few drinks or while watching a violent film. The tiniest negative emotion, such as being irritated or anxious, can also serve as a doorway through which the pain-body can return. The pain-body needs your unconsciousness. It cannot tolerate the light of Presence.

## THE PAIN-BODY AS AN AWAKENER

At first sight, it may seem that the pain-body is the greatest obstacle to the arising of a new consciousness in humanity. It occupies your mind, controls and distorts your thinking, disrupts your relationships, and feels like a dark cloud that occupies your entire energy field. It tends to make you unconscious, spiritually speaking, which means totally identified with mind and emotion. It makes you reactive, makes you say and do things that are designed to increase the unhappiness within yourself and the world.

As unhappiness increases, however, it also causes increasing disruption in your life. Perhaps the body can't take the stress anymore and develops an illness or some dysfunction. Perhaps you become involved in an accident, some huge conflict situation or drama that was caused by the pain-body's desire for something bad to happen, or you become the perpetrator of physical violence. Or it all becomes too much and you cannot live with your unhappy self anymore. The pain-body, of course, is part of that false self.

Whenever you get taken over by the pain-body, whenever you don't recognize it for what it is, it becomes part of your ego. Whatever you identify with turns into ego. The pain-body is one of the most powerful things the ego can identify with, just as the pain-body needs the ego to renew itself through it. That unholy alliance, however, eventually breaks down in those cases where the pain-body is so heavy that the egoic mind structures, instead of being strengthened by it, are becoming eroded by the continuous onslaught of the pain-body's energy charge, in the same way that an electronic device can be empowered by an electric current but also destroyed by it if the voltage is too high.

People with strong pain-bodies often reach a point where they feel their life is becoming unbearable, where they can't take any more pain, any more drama. One person expressed this by saying plainly and simply that she was "fed up with being unhappy." Some people may feel, as I did, that they cannot live with themselves anymore. Inner peace then becomes their first priority. Their acute emotional pain forces them to disidentify from the content of their minds and the mental-emotional structures that give birth to and perpetuate the unhappy me. They then know that neither their unhappy story nor the emotion they feel is who they are. They realize they are the knowing, not the known. Rather than pulling them into unconsciousness, the pain-body becomes their awakener, the decisive factor that forces them into a state of Presence.

However, due to the unprecedented influx of consciousness we are witnessing on the planet now, many people no longer need to go through the depth of acute suffering to be able to disidentify from the pain-body. Whenever they notice they have slipped back into a dysfunctional state, they are able to *choose* to step out of identification with thinking and emotion and enter the state of Presence. They relinquish resistance, become still and alert, one with what is, within and without.

The next step in human evolution is not inevitable, but for the first time in the history of our planet, it can be a conscious choice. Who is making that choice? You are. And who are you? Consciousness that has become conscious of itself.

## BREAKING FREE OF THE PAIN-BODY

A question people frequently ask is, "How long does it take to become free of the pain-body?" The answer is, of course, that it depends both on the density of an individual's pain-body as well as the degree or intensity of that individual's arising Presence. But it is not the pain-body, but identification with it that causes the suffering that you inflict on yourself and others. It is not the pain-body but identification with the pain-body that forces you to relive the past again and again and keeps you in a state of unconsciousness. So a more important question to ask would be this: "How long does it take to become free of identification with the pain-body?"

And the answer to that question is: It takes no time at all. When the pain-body is activated, know that what you are feeling is the pain-body in you. This knowing is all that is needed to break your identification with it. And when identification with it ceases, the transmutation begins. The knowing prevents the old emotion from rising up into your head and taking over not only the internal dialogue, but also your actions as well as interactions with other people. This means the pain-body cannot use you anymore and renew itself through you. The old emotion may then still live in you for a while and come up periodically. It may also still occasionally trick you into identifying with it again and thus obscure the knowing, but not for long. Not projecting the old emotion into situations means facing it directly within yourself. It may not be pleasant, but it won't kill you. Your Presence is more than capable of containing it. The emotion is not who you are.

When you feel the pain-body, don't fall into the error of thinking there is something wrong with you. Making yourself into a problem—the ego loves that. The knowing needs to be followed by accepting. Anything else will obscure it again. Accepting means you allow yourself to feel whatever it is you are feeling at that moment. It is part of the is-ness of the Now. You can't argue with *what is*. Well, you can, but if you do, you suffer. Through allowing, you become what you are: vast, spacious. You become whole. You are not a fragment anymore, which is how the ego perceives itself. Your true nature emerges, which is one with the nature of God.

Jesus points to this when he says, "Be ye whole, even as your Father in Heaven is whole."[1] The New Testament's "Be ye perfect" is a mistranslation of the original Greek word, which means whole. This is to say, you don't need to become whole, but *be* what you already are—with or without the pain-body.

## CHAPTER SEVEN

# Finding Who You Truly Are

*Gnothi Seauton*—Know Thyself. These words were inscribed above the entrance to the temple of Apollo at Delphi, site of the sacred Oracle. In ancient Greece, people would visit the Oracle hoping to find out what destiny had in store for them or what course of action to take in a particular situation. It is likely that most visitors read those words as they entered the building without realizing that they pointed to a deeper truth than anything the Oracle could possibly tell them. They may not have realized either that, no matter how great a revelation or how accurate the information they received, it would ultimately prove to be of no avail, would not save them from further unhappiness and self-created suffering, if they failed to find the truth that is concealed in that injunction—Know Thyself. What those words imply is this: Before you ask any other question, first ask the most fundamental question of your life: Who am I?

Unconscious people—and many remain unconscious, trapped in their egos throughout their lives—will quickly tell you who they are: their name, their occupation, their personal history, the shape or state of their body, and whatever else they identify with. Others may appear to be more evolved because they think of themselves as an immortal soul or divine spirit. But do they really know themselves, or have they just added some spiritual-sounding concepts to the content of their mind? Knowing yourself goes far deeper than the adoption of a set of ideas or beliefs. Spiritual ideas and beliefs may at best be helpful pointers, but in themselves they rarely have the power to dislodge the more firmly established core concepts of who you think you are, which are part of the conditioning of the human mind. Knowing yourself deeply has nothing to do with whatever ideas are floating around in your mind. Knowing yourself is to be rooted in Being, instead of lost in your mind.

## WHO YOU THINK YOU ARE

Your sense of who you are determines what you perceive as your needs and what matters to you in life—and whatever matters to you will have the power to upset and disturb you. You can use this as a criterion to find out how deeply you know yourself. What matters to you is not necessarily what you say or believe, but what your actions and reactions reveal as important and serious to you. So you may want to ask yourself the question: What are the things that upset and disturb me? If small things have the power to disturb you, then who you think you are is exactly that: small. That will be your unconscious belief. What are the small things? Ultimately all things are small things because all things are transient.

You might say, "I know I am an immortal spirit," or "I am tired of this mad world, and peace is all I want"—until the phone rings. Bad news: The stock market has collapsed; the deal may fall through; the car has been stolen; your mother-in-law has arrived; the trip is cancelled, the contract has been broken; your partner has left you; they demand more money; they say it's your fault. Suddenly there is a surge of anger, of anxiety. A harshness comes into your voice; "I can't take any more of this." You accuse and blame, attack, defend, or justify yourself, and it's all happening on autopilot. Something is obviously much more important to you now than the inner peace that a moment ago you said was all you wanted, and you're not an immortal spirit anymore either. The deal, the money, the contract, the loss or threat of loss are more important. To whom? To the immortal spirit that you said you are? No, to me. The small me that seeks security or fulfillment in things that are transient and gets anxious or angry because it fails to find it. Well, at least now you know who you really think you are.

If peace is really what you want, then you will choose peace. If peace mattered to you more than anything else and if you truly knew yourself to be spirit rather than a little me, you would remain nonreactive and absolutely alert when confronted with challenging people or situations. You would immediately accept the situation and thus become one with it rather than separate yourself from it. Then out of your alertness would come a response. Who you are (consciousness), not who you think you are (a small me), would be responding. It would be powerful and effective and would make no person or situation into an enemy.

The world always makes sure that you cannot fool yourself for long about who you really think you are by showing you what truly matters to you. How you react to people and situations, especially when challenges arise, is the best indicator of how deeply you know yourself.

The more limited, the more narrowly egoic the view of yourself, the more you will see, focus on, and react to the egoic limitations, the unconsciousness in others. Their "faults" or what you perceive as their faults become to you their identity. This means you will see only the ego in them and thus strengthen the ego in yourself. Instead of looking "through" the ego in others, you are looking "at" the ego. Who is looking at the ego? The ego in you.

Very unconscious people experience their own ego through its reflection in others. When you realize that what you react to in others is also in you (and sometimes only in you), you begin to become aware of your own ego. At that stage, you may also realize that you were doing to others what you thought others were doing to you. You cease seeing yourself as a victim.

You are not the ego, so when you become aware of the ego in you, it does not mean you know who you are—it means you know who you are *not*. But it is through knowing who you are not that the greatest obstacle to truly knowing yourself is removed.

Nobody can tell you who you are. It would just be another concept, so it would not change you. *Who you are* requires no belief. In fact, every belief is an obstacle. It does not even require your realization, since you already are who you are. But without realization, who you are does not shine forth into this world. It remains in the unmanifested which is, of course, your true home. You are then like an apparently poor person who does not know he has a bank account with $100 million in it and so his wealth remains an unexpressed potential.

## ABUNDANCE

Who you think you are is also intimately connected with how you see yourself treated by others. Many people complain that others do not treat them well enough. "I don't get any respect, attention, recognition, acknowledgment," they say. "I'm being taken for granted." When people are kind, they suspect hidden motives. "Others want to manipulate me, take advantage of me. Nobody loves me."

Who they think they are is this: "I am a needy 'little me' whose needs are not being met." This basic misperception of who they are creates dysfunction in all their relationships. They believe they have nothing to give and that the world or other people are withholding from them what they need. Their entire reality is based on an illusory sense of who they are. It sabotages situations, mars all relationships. If the thought of lack—whether it be money, recognition, or love—has become part of who you think you are, you will always experience lack. Rather than acknowledge the good that is already in your life, all you see is lack. Acknowledging the good that is already in your life is the foundation for all abundance. The fact is: Whatever you think the world is withholding from you, you are withholding from the world. You are withholding it because deep down you think you are small and that you have nothing to give.

Try this for a couple of weeks and see how it changes

your reality: Whatever you think people are withholding from you—praise, appreciation, assistance, loving care, and so on—give it to them. You don't have it? Just act as if you had it, and it will come. Then, soon after you start giving, you will start receiving. You cannot receive what you don't give. Outflow determines inflow. Whatever you think the world is withholding from you, you already have, but unless you allow it to flow out, you won't even know that you have it. This includes abundance. The law that outflow determines inflow is expressed by Jesus in this powerful image: "Give and it will be given to you. Good measure, pressed down, shaken together, running over, will be put into your lap."[1]

The source of all abundance is not outside you. It is part of who you are. However, start by acknowledging and recognizing abundance without. See the fullness of life all around you. The warmth of the sun on your skin, the display of magnificent flowers outside a florist's shop, biting into a succulent fruit, or getting soaked in an abundance of water falling from the sky. The fullness of life is there at every step. The acknowledgment of that abundance that is all around you awakens the dormant abundance within. Then let it flow out. When you smile at a stranger, there is already a minute outflow of energy. You become a giver. Ask yourself often: "What can I give here; how can I be of service to this person, this situation?" You don't need to own anything to feel abundant, although if you feel abundant consistently things will almost certainly come to you. Abundance comes only to those who already have it. It sounds almost unfair, but of course it isn't. It is a universal law. Both abundance and scarcity are inner states that manifest as your reality. Jesus puts it like this: "For to the one who has, more will be given, and from the one who has not, even what he has will be taken away."[2]

## KNOWING YOURSELF AND KNOWING *ABOUT* YOURSELF

You may not want to know yourself because you are afraid of what you may find out. Many people have a secret fear that they are bad. But nothing you can find out about yourself is you. Nothing you can know *about* you is you.

While some people do not want to know who they are because of fear, others have an insatiable curiosity about themselves and want to find out more and more. You may be so fascinated with yourself that you spend years in psychoanalysis, delve into every aspect of your childhood, uncover secret fears and desires, and find layers upon layers of complexity in the makeup of your personality and character. After ten years, the therapist may get tired of you and your story and tell you that your analysis is now complete. Perhaps he sends you away with a five-thousand-page dossier. "This is all about you. This is who you are." As you carry the heavy file home, the initial satisfaction of at last

knowing yourself gives way quickly to a feeling of incompleteness and a lurking suspicion that there must be more to
who you are than this. And indeed there is more—not perhaps in quantitative terms of more facts but in the qualita-
tive dimension of depth.

There is nothing wrong with psychoanalysis or finding
out about your past as long as you don't confuse knowing
*about* yourself with knowing yourself. The five-thousand-
page dossier is *about* yourself: the content of your mind
which is conditioned by the past. Whatever you learn
through psychoanalysis or self-observation is *about* you. It is
not you. It is content, not essence. Going beyond ego is
stepping out of content. Knowing yourself is being yourself, and being yourself is ceasing to identify with content.

Most people define themselves through the content of
their lives. Whatever you perceive, experience, do, think,
or feel is content. Content is what absorbs most people's attention entirely, and it is what they identify with. When
you think or say, "my life," you are not referring to the life
that you *are* but the life that you *have*, or seem to have. You
are referring to content—your age, health, relationships, fi-
nances, work and living situation, as well as your mental-
emotional state. The inner and outer circumstances of your
life, your past and your future, all belong to the realm of
content—as do events, that is to say, anything that happens.

What is there other than content? That which enables
the content to be—the inner space of consciousness.

## CHAOS AND HIGHER ORDER

When you know yourself only through content, you will also think you know what is good or bad for you. You differentiate between events that are "good for me" and those that are "bad." This is a fragmented perception of the wholeness of life in which everything is interconnected, in which every event has its necessary place and function within the totality. The totality, however, is more than the surface appearance of things, more than the sum total of its parts, more than whatever your life or the world contains.

Behind the sometimes seemingly random or even chaotic succession of events in our lives as well as in the world lies concealed the unfolding of a higher order and purpose. This is beautifully expressed in the Zen saying "The snow falls, each flake in its appropriate place." We can never understand this higher order through thinking about it because whatever we think about is content; whereas, the higher order emanates from the formless realm of consciousness, from universal intelligence. But we can glimpse it, and more than that, align ourselves with it, which means be conscious participants in the unfolding of that higher purpose.

When we go into a forest that has not been interfered with by man, our thinking mind will see only disorder and chaos all around us. It won't even be able to differentiate between life (good) and death (bad) anymore since everywhere new life grows out of rotting and decaying matter. Only if we are still enough inside and the noise of thinking subsides can we become aware that there is a hidden harmony here, a sacredness, a higher order in which everything has its perfect place and could not be other than what it is and the way it is.

The mind is more comfortable in a landscaped park because it has been planned through thought; it has not grown organically. There is an order here that the mind can understand. In the forest, there is an incomprehensible order that to the mind looks like chaos. It is beyond the mental categories of good and bad. You cannot understand it through thought, but you can sense it when you let go of thought, become still and alert, and don't try to understand or explain. Only then can you be aware of the sacredness of the forest. As soon as you sense that hidden harmony, that sacredness, you realize you are not separate from it, and when you realize that, you become a conscious participant in it. In this way, nature can help you become realigned with the wholeness of life.

## GOOD AND BAD

At some point in their lives, most people become aware that there is not only birth, growth, success, good health, pleasure, and winning, but also loss, failure, sickness, old age, decay, pain, and death. Conventionally these are labeled "good" and "bad," order and disorder. The "meaning" of people's lives is usually associated with what they term the "good," but the good is continually threatened by collapse, breakdown, disorder; threatened by meaninglessness and the "bad," when explanations fail and life ceases to make sense. Sooner or later, disorder will irrupt into everyone's life no matter how many insurance policies he or she has. It may come in the form of loss or accident, sickness, disability, old age, death. However, the irruption of disorder into a person's life, and the resultant collapse of a mentally defined meaning, can become the opening into a higher order.

"The wisdom of this world is folly with God," says the Bible.[3] What is the wisdom of this world? The movement of thought, and meaning that is defined exclusively by thought.

Thinking isolates a situation or event and calls it good or bad, as if it had a separate existence. Through excessive reliance on thinking, reality becomes fragmented. This fragmentation is an illusion, but it seems very real while you are trapped in it. And yet the universe is an indivisible whole in which all things are interconnected, in which nothing exists in isolation.

The deeper interconnectedness of all things and events implies that the mental labels of "good" and "bad" are ultimately illusory. They always imply a limited perspective and so are true only relatively and temporarily. This is illustrated in the story of a wise man who won an expensive car in a lottery. His family and friends were very happy for him and came to celebrate. "Isn't it great!" they said. "You are so lucky." The man smiled and said, "Maybe." For a few weeks he enjoyed driving the car. Then one day a drunken driver crashed into his new car at an intersection and he ended up in the hospital, with multiple injuries. His family and friends came to see him and said, "That was really unfortunate." Again the man smiled and said, "Maybe." While he was still in the hospital, one night there was a landslide and his house fell into the sea. Again his friends came the next day and said, "Weren't you lucky to have been here in hospital." Again he said, "Maybe."

The wise man's "maybe" signifies a refusal to judge anything that happens. Instead of judging what is, he accepts it and so enters into conscious alignment with the higher order. He knows that often it is impossible for the mind to understand what place or purpose a seemingly random event has in the tapestry of the whole. But there are no random events, nor are there events or things that exist by and for themselves, in isolation. The atoms that make up your body were once forged inside stars, and the causes of even the smallest event are virtually infinite and connected with the whole in incomprehensible ways. If you wanted to trace back the cause of any event, you would have to go back all the way to the beginning of creation. The cosmos is not chaotic. The very word *cosmos* means order. But this is not an order the human mind can ever comprehend, although it can sometimes glimpse it.

## NOT MINDING WHAT HAPPENS

J. Krishnamurti, the great Indian philosopher and spiritual teacher, spoke and traveled almost continuously all over the world for more than fifty years attempting to convey through words—which are content—that which is beyond words, beyond content. At one of his talks in the later part of his life, he surprised his audience by asking, "Do you want to know my secret?" Everyone became very alert. Many people in the audience had been coming to listen to him for twenty or thirty years and still failed to grasp the essence of his teaching. Finally, after all these years, the master would give them the key to understanding. "This is my secret," he said. "I don't mind what happens."

He did not elaborate, and so I suspect most of his audience were even more perplexed than before. The implications of this simple statement, however, are profound.

When I don't mind what happens, what does that imply? It implies that internally I am in alignment with what happens. "What happens," of course, refers to the suchness of this moment, which always already is as it is. It refers to content, the form that this moment—the only moment there ever is—takes. To be in alignment with *what is* means to be in a relationship of inner nonresistance with what happens. It means not to label it mentally as good or bad, but to let it be. Does this mean you can no longer take action to bring about change in your life? On the contrary. When the basis for your actions is inner alignment with the present moment, your actions become empowered by the intelligence of Life itself.

## IS THAT SO?

The Zen Master Hakuin lived in a town in Japan. He was held in high regard and many people came to him for spiritual teaching. Then it happened that the teenage daughter of his next-door neighbor became pregnant. When being questioned by her angry and scolding parents as to the identity of the father, she finally told them that he was Hakuin, the Zen Master. In great anger the parents rushed over to Hakuin and told him with much shouting and accusing that their daughter had confessed that he was the father. All he replied was, "Is that so?"

News of the scandal spread throughout the town and beyond. The Master lost his reputation. This did not trouble him. Nobody came to see him anymore. He remained unmoved. When the child was born, the parents brought the baby to Hakuin. "You are the father, so you look after him." The Master took loving care of the child. A year later, the mother remorsefully confessed to her parents that the real father of the child was the young man who worked at the butcher shop. In great distress they went to see Hakuin to apologize and ask for forgiveness. "We are really sorry. We have come to take the baby back. Our daughter confessed that you are not the father." "Is that so?" is all he would say as he handed the baby over to them.

The Master responds to falsehood and truth, bad news and good news, in exactly the same way: "Is that so?" He allows the form of the moment, good or bad, to be as it is and so does not become a participant in human drama. To him there is only this moment, and this moment is as it is. Events are not personalized. He is nobody's victim. He is so completely at one with what happens that what happens has no power over him anymore. Only if you resist what happens are you at the mercy of what happens, and the world will determine your happiness and unhappiness.

The baby is looked after with loving care. Bad turns into good through the power of nonresistance. Always responding to what the present moment requires, he lets go of the baby when it is time to do so.

Imagine briefly how the ego would have reacted during the various stages of the unfolding of these events.


## THE EGO AND THE PRESENT MOMENT

The most important, the primordial relationship in your life is your relationship with the Now, or rather with whatever form the Now takes, that is to say, what is or what happens. If your relationship with the Now is dysfunctional, that dysfunction will be reflected in every relationship and every situation you encounter. The ego could be defined simply in this way: a dysfunctional relationship with the present moment. It is at this moment that you can decide what kind of relationship you want to have with the present moment.

Once you have reached a certain level of consciousness, (and if you are reading this, you almost certainly have), you are able to decide what kind of a relationship you want to have with the present moment. Do I want the present moment to be my friend or my enemy? The present moment is inseparable from life, so you are really deciding what kind of a relationship you want to have with life. Once you have decided you want the present moment to be your friend, it is up to you to make the first move: Become friendly toward it, welcome it no matter in what disguise it comes, and soon you will see the results. Life becomes friendly toward you; people become helpful, circumstances cooperative. One decision changes your entire reality. But that one decision you have to make again and again and again—until it becomes natural to live in such a way.

The decision to make the present moment into your friend is the end of the ego. The ego can never be in alignment with the present moment, which is to say, aligned with life, since its very nature compels it to ignore, resist, or devalue the Now. Time is what the ego lives on. The stronger the ego, the more time takes over your life. Almost every thought you think is then concerned with past or future, and your sense of self depends on the past for your identity and on the future for its fulfillment. Fear, anxiety, expectation, regret, guilt, anger are the dysfunctions of the time-bound state of consciousness.

There are three ways in which the ego will treat the present moment: as a means to an end, as an obstacle, or as an enemy. Let us look at them in turn, so that when this pattern operates in you, you can recognize it and—decide again.

To the ego, the present moment is, at best, only useful as a means to an end. It gets you to some future moment that is considered more important, even though the future never comes except as the present moment and is therefore never more than a thought in your head. In other words, you are never fully here because you are always busy trying to get elsewhere.

When this pattern becomes more pronounced, and this is very common, the present moment is regarded and treated as if it were an obstacle to be overcome. This is where impatience, frustration, and stress arise, and in our culture, it is many people's everyday reality, their normal state. Life, which is now, is seen as a "problem," and you come to inhabit a world of problems that all need to be solved before you can be happy, fulfilled, or really start living—or so you think. The problem is: For every problem that is solved, another one pops up. As long as the present moment is seen as an obstacle, there can be no end to problems. "I'll be whatever you want me to be," says Life or the Now. "I'll treat you the way you treat me. If you see me as a problem, I will be a problem to you. If you treat me as an obstacle, I will be an obstacle."

At worst, and this is also very common, the present moment is treated as if it were an enemy. When you hate what you are doing, complain about your surroundings, curse things that are happening or have happened, or when your internal dialogue consists of shoulds and shouldn'ts, of blaming and accusing, then you are arguing with what *is*, arguing with that which is always already the case. You are making Life into an enemy and Life says, "War is what you want, and war is what you get." External reality, which always reflects back to you your inner state, is then experienced as hostile.

A vital question to ask yourself frequently is: What is my relationship with the present moment? Then become alert to find out the answer. Am I treating the Now as no more than a means to an end? Do I see it as an obstacle? Am I making it into an enemy? Since the present moment is all you ever have, since Life is inseparable from the Now, what the question really means is: What is my relationship with Life? This question is an excellent way of unmasking the ego in you and bringing you into the state of Presence. Although the question doesn't embody the absolute truth (ultimately, I and the present moment are one), it is a useful pointer in the right direction. Ask yourself it often until you don't need it anymore.

How do you go beyond a dysfunctional relationship with the present moment? The most important thing is to see it in yourself, in your thoughts and actions. In the moment of seeing, of noticing that your relationship with the Now is dysfunctional, you are present. The seeing is the arising Presence. The moment you see the dysfunction, it begins to dissolve. Some people laugh out loud when they see this. With the seeing comes the power of choice—the choice of saying yes to the Now, of making it into your friend.

## THE PARADOX OF TIME

On the surface, the present moment is "what happens." Since what happens changes continuously, it seems that every day of your life consists of thousands of moments in which different things happen. Time is seen as the endless succession of moments, some "good," some "bad." Yet, if you look more closely, that is to say, through your own immediate experience, you find that there are not many moments at all. You discover that there is only ever *this moment*. Life is always now. Your entire life unfolds in this constant Now. Even past or future moments only exist when you remember or anticipate them, and you do so by thinking about them in the only moment there is: this one.

Why does it appear then as if there were many moments? Because the present moment is confused with what happens, confused with content. The space of Now is confused with what happens in that space. The confusion of the present moment with content gives rise not only to the illusion of time, but also to the illusion of ego.

There is a paradox here. On the one hand, how can we deny the reality of time? You need it to go from here to there, to prepare a meal, build a house, read this book. You need time to grow up, to learn new things. Whatever you do seems to take time. Everything is subject to it and eventually "this bloody tyrant time," as Shakespeare calls it, is going to kill you. You could compare it to a raging river that drags you along with it, or a fire in which everything is consumed.

I recently met some old friends, a family I had not seen in a long time, and I was shocked when I saw them. I almost asked, "Are you ill? What happened? Who did this to you?" The mother, who walked with a cane, seemed to have shrunk in size, her face shriveled like an old apple. The daughter, who had been full of energy, enthusiasm, and the expectations of youth when I last saw her, seemed worn out, tired after bringing up three children. Then I remembered: Almost thirty years had passed since we last met. Time had done this to them. And I'm sure they were just as shocked when they saw me.

Everything seems to be subject to time, yet it all happens in the Now. That is the paradox. Wherever you look, there is plenty of *circumstantial* evidence for the reality of time—a rotting apple, your face in the bathroom mirror compared to your face in a photo taken thirty years ago—yet you never find any *direct* evidence, you never experience time itself. You only ever experience the present moment, or rather what happens in it. If you go by direct evidence only, then there is no time, and the Now is all there ever is.

## ELIMINATING TIME

You cannot make the egoless state into a future goal and then work toward it. All you get is more dissatisfaction, more inner conflict, because it will always seem that you have not arrived yet, have not "attained" that state yet. When freedom from ego is your goal for the future, you give yourself more time, and more time means more ego. Look carefully to find out if your spiritual search is a disguised form of ego. Even trying to get rid of your "self" can be a disguised search for more if the getting rid of your "self" is made into a future goal. Giving yourself more time is precisely this: giving your "self" more time. Time, that is to say, past and future, is what the false mind-made self, the ego, lives on, and time is in your mind. It isn't something that has an objective existence "out there." It is a mind-structure needed for sensory perception, indispensable for practical purposes, but the greatest hindrance to knowing yourself. Time is the horizontal dimension of life, the surface layer of reality. Then there is the vertical dimension of depth, accessible to you only through the portal of the present moment.

So instead of adding time to yourself, remove time. The elimination of time from your consciousness is the elimination of ego. It is the only true spiritual practice.

When we speak of the elimination of time, we are, of course, not referring to clock time, which is the use of time for practical purposes, such as making an appointment or planning a trip. It would be almost impossible to function in this world without clock time. What we are speaking of is the elimination of psychological time, which is the egoic mind's endless preoccupation with past and future and its unwillingness to be one with life by living in alignment with the inevitable *isness* of the present moment.

Whenever a habitual no to life turns into a yes, whenever you allow this moment to be as it is, you dissolve time as well as ego. For the ego to survive, it must make time—past and future—more important than the present moment. The ego cannot tolerate becoming friendly with the present moment, except briefly just after it got what it wanted. But nothing can satisfy the ego for long. As long as it runs your life, there are two ways of being unhappy. Not getting what you want is one. Getting what you want is the other.

Whatever is or happens is the form that the Now takes. As long as you resist it internally, form, that is to say, the world, is an impenetrable barrier that separates you from who you are beyond form, separates you from the formless one Life that you are. When you bring an inner yes to the form the Now takes, that very form becomes a doorway into the formless. The separation between the world and God dissolves.

When you react against the form that Life takes at this moment, when you treat the Now as a means, an obstacle, or an enemy, you strengthen your own form identity, the ego. Hence the ego's reactivity. What is reactivity? Becoming addicted to reaction. The more reactive you are, the more entangled you become with form. The more identified with form, the stronger the ego. Your Being then does not shine through form anymore—or only barely.

Through nonresistance to form, that in you which is beyond form emerges as an all-encompassing Presence, a silent power far greater than your short-lived form identity, the person. It is more deeply who you are than anything in the world of form.

## THE DREAMER AND THE DREAM

Nonresistance is the key to the greatest power in the universe. Through it, consciousness (spirit) is freed from its imprisonment in form. Inner nonresistance to form— whatever is or happens—is a denial of the absolute reality of form. Resistance makes the world and the things of the world appear more real, more solid, and more lasting than they are, including your own form identity, the ego. It endows the world and the ego with a heaviness and an absolute importance that makes you take yourself and the world very seriously. The play of form is then misperceived as a struggle for survival, and when that is your perception, it becomes your reality.

The many things that happen, the many forms that life takes on, are of an ephemeral nature. They are all fleeting. Things, bodies and egos, events, situations, thoughts, emotions, desires, ambitions, fears, drama . . . they come, pretend to be all-important, and before you know it they are gone, dissolved into the no-thingness out of which they came. Were they ever real? Were they ever more than a dream, the dream of form?

When we wake up in the morning, the night's dream dissolves, and we say, "Oh, it was only a dream. It wasn't real." But something in the dream must have been real otherwise it could not be. When death approaches, we may look back on our life and wonder if it was just another dream. Even now you may look back on last year's vacation or yesterday's drama and see that it is very similar to last night's dream.

There is the dream, and there is the dreamer of the dream. The dream is a short-lived play of forms. It is the world—relatively real but not absolutely real. Then there is the dreamer, the absolute reality in which the forms come and go. The dreamer is not the person. The person is part of the dream. The dreamer is the substratum in which the dream appears, that which makes the dream possible. It is the absolute behind the relative, the timeless behind time, the consciousness in and behind form. The dreamer is consciousness itself—who you are.

To awaken within the dream is our purpose now. When we are awake within the dream, the ego-created earth-drama comes to an end and a more benign and wondrous dream arises. This is the new earth.

## GOING BEYOND LIMITATION

In each person's life there comes a time when he or she pursues growth and expansion on the level of form. This is when you strive to overcome limitation such as physical weakness or financial scarcity, when you acquire new skills and knowledge, or through creative action bring something new into this world that is life-enhancing for yourself as well as others. This may be a piece of music or a work of art, a book, a service you provide, a function you perform, a business or organization that you set up or make a vital contribution to.

When you are present, when your attention is fully in the Now, that Presence will flow into and transform what you do. There will be quality and power in it. You are present when what you are doing is not primarily a means to an end (money, prestige, winning) but fulfilling in itself, when there is joy and aliveness in what you do. And, of course, you cannot be present unless you become friendly with the present moment. That is the basis for effective action, uncontaminated by negativity.

Form means limitation. We are here not only to experience limitation, but also to grow in consciousness by going beyond limitation. Some limitations can be overcome on an external level. There may be other limitations in your life that you have to learn to live with. They can only be overcome internally. Everyone will encounter them sooner or later. Those limitations either keep you trapped in egoic reaction, which means intense unhappiness, or you rise above them internally by uncompromising surrender to what is. That is what they are here to teach. The surrendered state of consciousness opens up the vertical dimension in your life, the dimension of depth. Something will then come forth from that dimension into this world, something of infinite value that otherwise would have remained unmanifested. Some people who surrendered to severe limitation become healers or spiritual teachers. Others work selflessly to lessen human suffering or bring some creative gift into this world.

In the late seventies, I would have lunch every day with one or two friends in the cafeteria of the graduate center at Cambridge University, where I was studying. A man in a wheelchair would sometimes sit at a nearby table, usually accompanied by three or four people. One day, when he was sitting at a table directly opposite me, I could not help but look at him more closely, and I was shocked by what I saw. He seemed almost totally paralyzed. His body was emaciated, his head permanently slumped forward. One of the people accompanying him was carefully putting food in his mouth, a great deal of which would fall out again and be caught on a small plate another man was holding under his chin. Occasionally the wheelchair-bound man would produce unintelligible croaking sounds, and someone would hold an ear close to his mouth and then amazingly would interpret what he was trying to say.

Later I asked my friend whether he knew who he was. "Of course," he said, "he is a professor of mathematics, and the people with him are his graduate students. He has motor neuron disease that progressively paralyzes every part of the body. He has been given five years at the most. It must be the most dreadful fate that can befall a human being."

A few weeks later, as I was leaving the building, he was coming in, and when I held the door open for his electric wheelchair to come through, our eyes met. With surprise I saw that his eyes were clear. There was no trace in them of unhappiness. I knew immediately he had relinquished resistance; he was living in surrender.

A number of years later when buying a newspaper at a kiosk, I was amazed to see him on the front page of a popular international news magazine. Not only was he still alive, but he had by then become the world's most famous theoretical physicist, Stephen Hawking. There was a beautiful line in the article that confirmed what I had sensed when I had looked into his eyes many years earlier. Commenting upon his life, he said (now with the help of the voice synthesizer), "Who could have wished for more?"

## THE JOY OF BEING

Unhappiness or negativity is a disease on our planet. What pollution is on the outer level is negativity on the inner. It is everywhere, not just in places where people don't have enough, but even more so where they have more than enough. Is that surprising? No. The affluent world is even more deeply identified with form, more lost in content, more trapped in ego.

People believe themselves to be dependent on what happens for their happiness, that is to say, dependent on form. They don't realize that what happens is the most unstable thing in the universe. It changes constantly. They look upon the present moment as either marred by something that has happened and shouldn't have or as deficient because of something that has not happened but should have. And so they miss the deeper perfection that is inherent in life itself, a perfection that is always already here, that lies beyond what is happening or not happening, beyond form.

Accept the present moment and find the perfection that is deeper than any form and untouched by time.

The joy of Being, which is the only true happiness, cannot come to you through any form, possession, achievement, person, or event—through anything that happens. That joy cannot *come* to you—ever. It emanates from the formless dimension within you, from consciousness itself and thus is one with who you are.

## ALLOWING THE DIMINISHMENT OF THE EGO

The ego is always on guard against any kind of perceived diminishment. Automatic ego-repair mechanisms come into effect to restore the mental form of "me." When someone blames or criticizes me, that to the ego is a diminishment of self, and it will immediately attempt to repair its diminished sense of self through self-justification, defense, or blaming. Whether the other person is right or wrong is irrelevant to the ego. It is much more interested in self-preservation than in the truth. This is the preservation of the psychological form of "me." Even such a normal thing as shouting something back when another driver calls you "idiot" is an automatic and unconscious ego-repair mechanism. One of the most common ego-repair mechanisms is anger, which causes a temporary but huge ego inflation. All repair mechanisms make perfect sense to the ego but are actually dysfunctional. Those that are most extreme in their dysfunction are physical violence and self-delusion in the form of grandiose fantasies.

A powerful spiritual practice is consciously to allow the diminishment of ego when it happens without attempting to restore it. I recommend that you experiment with this from time to time. For example, when someone criticizes you, blames you, or calls you names, instead of immediately retaliating or defending yourself—do nothing. Allow the self-image to remain diminished and become alert to what that feels like deep inside you. For a few seconds, it may feel uncomfortable, as if you had shrunk in size. Then you may sense an inner spaciousness that feels intensely alive. You haven't been diminished at all. In fact, you have expanded. You may then come to an amazing realization: When you are seemingly diminished in some way and remain in absolute nonreaction, not just externally but also internally, you realize that nothing real has been diminished, that through becoming "less," you become more. When you no longer defend or attempt to strengthen the form of yourself, you step out of identification with form, with mental self-image. Through becoming less (in the ego's perception), you in fact undergo an expansion and make room for Being to come forward. True power, who you are beyond form, can then shine through the apparently weakened form. This is what Jesus means when he says, "Deny yourself" or "Turn the other cheek."

This does not mean, of course, that you invite abuse or turn yourself into a victim of unconscious people. Sometimes a situation may demand that you tell someone to "back off" in no uncertain terms. Without egoic defensiveness, there will be power behind your words, yet no reactive force. If necessary, you can also say no to someone firmly and clearly, and it will be what I call a "high-quality no" that is free of all negativity.

If you are content with being nobody in particular, content not to stand out, you align yourself with the power of the universe. What looks like weakness to the ego is in fact the only true strength. This spiritual truth is diametrically opposed to the values of our contemporary culture and the way it conditions people to behave.

Instead of trying to be a mountain, teaches the ancient *Tao Te Ching*, "Be the valley of the universe."[4] In this way, you are restored to wholeness and so "all things will come to you."[5]

Similarly, Jesus, in one of his parables, teaches that "When you are invited, go and sit in the lowest place so that when your host comes, he may say to you, friend, move up higher. Then you will be honored in the presence of all who sit at table with you. For everyone who exalts himself will be humbled, and he who humbles himself will be exalted."[6]

Another aspect of this practice is to refrain from attempting to strengthen the self by showing off, wanting to

stand out, be special, make an impression, or demand attention. It may include occasionally refraining from expressing
your opinion when everybody is expressing his or hers, and
seeing what that feels like.

## AS WITHOUT, SO WITHIN

When you look up at the clear sky at night, you may easily
realize a truth at once utterly simple and extraordinarily
profound. What is it that you see? The moon, planets, stars,
the luminous band of the Milky Way, perhaps a comet or
even the neighboring Andromeda Galaxy two million light
years away. Yes, but if you simplify even more, what do you
see? Objects floating in space. So what does the universe
consist of? Objects and space.

If you don't become speechless when looking out into
space on a clear night, you are not really looking, not aware
of the totality of what is there. You are probably only looking at the objects and perhaps seeking to name them. If you
have ever experienced a sense of awe when looking into
space, perhaps even felt a deep reverence in the face of this
incomprehensible mystery, it means you must have relinquished for a moment your desire to explain and label and
have become aware not only of the objects in space but of
the infinite depth of space itself. You must have become
still enough inside to notice the vastness in which these
countless worlds exist. The feeling of awe is not derived

from the fact that there are billions of worlds out there, but the depth that contains them all.

You cannot see space, of course, nor can you hear, touch, taste, or smell it, so how do you even know it exists? This logical-sounding question already contains a fundamental error. The essence of space is no-thingness, so it doesn't "exist" in the normal sense of the word. Only things—forms—exist. Even calling it space can be misleading because by naming it, you make it into an object.

Let us put it like this: There is something within you that has an affinity with space; that is why you can be aware of it. Aware of it? That's not totally true either because how can you be aware of space if there is nothing there to be aware of?

The answer is both simple and profound. When you are aware of space, you are not really aware of anything, except awareness itself—the inner space of consciousness. Through you, the universe is becoming aware of itself!

When the eye finds nothing to see, that no-thingness is perceived as space. When the ear finds nothing to hear, that no-thingness is perceived as stillness. When the senses, which are designed to perceive form, meet an absence of form, the formless consciousness that lies behind perception and makes all perception, all experience, possible, is no longer obscured by form. When you contemplate the unfathomable depth of space or listen to the silence in the

early hours just before sunrise, something within you resonates with it as if in recognition. You then sense the vast
depth of space as your own depth, and you know that precious stillness that has no form to be more deeply who you
are than any of the things that make up the content of
your life.

The Upanishads, the ancient scriptures of India, point to
the same truth with these words:

> What cannot be seen with the eye, but that whereby the
> eye can see: know that alone to be Brahman the Spirit
> and not what people here adore. What cannot be heard
> with the ear but that whereby the ear can hear: know
> that alone to be Brahman the Spirit and not what people
> here adore. . . . What cannot be thought with the mind,
> but that whereby the mind can think: know that alone
> to be Brahman the Spirit and not what people here
> adore.[7]

God, the scripture is saying, is formless consciousness
and the essence of who you are. Everything else is form, is
"what people here adore."

The twofold reality of the universe, which consists of
things and space—thingness and no-thingness—is also your
own. A sane, balanced, and fruitful human life is a dance
between the two dimensions that make up reality: form and
space. Most people are so identified with the dimension of

form, with sense perceptions, thoughts, and emotion, that the vital hidden half is missing from their lives. Their identification with form keeps them trapped in ego.

What you see, hear, feel, touch, or think about is only one half of reality, so to speak. It is form. In the teaching of Jesus, it is simply called "the world," and the other dimension is "the kingdom of heaven or eternal life."

Just as space enables all things to exist and just as without silence there could be no sound, you would not exist without the vital formless dimension that is the essence of who you are. We could say "God" if the word had not been so misused. I prefer to call it Being. Being is prior to existence. Existence is form, content, "what happens." Existence is the foreground of life; Being is the background, as it were.

The collective disease of humanity is that people are so engrossed in what happens, so hypnotized by the world of fluctuating forms, so absorbed in the content of their lives, they have forgotten the essence, that which is beyond content, beyond form, beyond thought. They are so consumed by time that they have forgotten eternity, which is their origin, their home, their destiny. Eternity is the living reality of who you are.

Some years ago when visiting China, I came upon a stupa on a mountaintop near Guilin. It had writing embossed in gold on it, and I asked my Chinese host what it meant. "It means 'Buddha,' " he said. "Why are there two characters rather than one?" I asked. "One," he explained, means 'man.' The other means 'no.' And the two together means 'Buddha.' " I stood there in awe. The character for Buddha already contained the whole teaching of the Buddha, and for those who have eyes to see, the secret of life. Here are the two dimensions that make up reality, thingness and no-thingness, form and the denial of form, which is the recognition that form is not who you are.

## CHAPTER EIGHT

# The Discovery of Inner Space

According to an ancient Sufi story, there lived a king in some Middle Eastern land who was continuously torn between happiness and despondency. The slightest thing would cause him great upset or provoke an intense reaction, and his happiness would quickly turn into disappointment and despair. A time came when the king finally got tired of himself and of life, and he began to seek a way out. He sent for a wise man who lived in his kingdom and who was reputed to be enlightened. When the wise man came, the king said to him, "I want to be like you. Can you give me something that will bring balance, serenity, and wisdom into my life? I will pay any price you ask."

The wise man said, "I may be able to help you. But the

price is so great that your entire kingdom would not be sufficient payment for it. Therefore it will be a gift to you if you will honor it." The king gave his assurances, and the wise man left.

A few weeks later, he returned and handed the king an ornate box carved in jade. The king opened the box and found a simple gold ring inside. Some letters were inscribed on the ring. The inscription read: *This, too, will pass.* "What is the meaning of this?" asked the king. The wise man said, "Wear this ring always. Whatever happens, before you call it good or bad, touch this ring and read the inscription. That way, you will always be at peace."

*This, too, will pass.* What is it about these simple words that makes them so powerful? Looking at it superficially, it would seem while those words may provide some comfort in a bad situation, they would also diminish the enjoyment of the good things in life. "Don't be too happy, because it won't last." This seems to be what they are saying when applied in a situation that is perceived as good.

The full import of these words becomes clear when we consider them in the context of two other stories that we encountered earlier. The story of the Zen Master whose only response was always "Is that so?" shows the good that comes through inner nonresistance to events, that is to say, being at one with what happens. The story of the man whose comment was invariably a laconic "Maybe" illustrates the wisdom of nonjudgment, and the story of the ring points to the fact of impermanence which, when recognized, leads to nonattachment. Nonresistance, nonjudgment, and nonattachment are the three aspects of true freedom and enlightened living.

Those words inscribed on the ring are not telling you that you should not enjoy the good in your life, nor are they merely meant to provide some comfort in times of suffering. They have a deeper purpose: to make you aware of the fleetingness of every situation, which is due to the transience of all forms—good or bad. When you become aware of the transience of all forms, your attachment to them lessens, and you disidentify from them to some extent. Being detached does not mean that you cannot enjoy the good that the world has to offer. In fact, you enjoy it more. Once you see and accept the transience of all things and the inevitability of change, you can enjoy the pleasures of the world while they last without fear of loss or anxiety about the future. When you are detached, you gain a higher vantage point from which to view the events in your life instead of being trapped inside them. You become like an astronaut who sees the planet Earth surrounded by the vastness of space and realizes a paradoxical truth: The earth is precious and at the same time insignificant. The recognition that *This, too, will pass* brings detachment and with detachment another dimension comes into your life—inner space. Through detachment, as well as nonjudgment and inner nonresistance, you gain access to that dimension.

When you are no longer totally identified with forms, consciousness—who you are—becomes freed from its imprisonment in form. This freedom is the arising of inner space. It comes as a stillness, a subtle peace deep within you, even in the face of something seemingly bad. *This, too, will pass.* Suddenly, there is space around the event. There is also space around the emotional highs and lows, even around pain. And above all, there is space between your thoughts. And from that space emanates a peace that is not "of this world," because this world is form, and the peace is space. This is the peace of God.

Now you can enjoy and honor the things of this world without giving them an importance and significance they don't have. You can participate in the dance of creation and be active without attachment to outcome and without placing unreasonable demands upon the world: Fulfill me, make me happy, make me feel safe, tell me who I am. The world cannot give you those things, and when you no longer have such expectations, all self-created suffering comes to an end. All such suffering is due to an overvaluation of form and an unawareness of the dimension of inner space. When that dimension is present in your life, you can enjoy things, experiences, and the pleasures of the senses without losing yourself in them, without inner attachment to them, that is to say, without becoming addicted to the world.

The words *This, too, will pass* are pointers toward reality.

In pointing to the impermanence of all forms, by implication, they are also pointing to the eternal. Only the eternal in you can recognize the impermanent as impermanent.

When the dimension of space is lost or rather not known, the things of the world assume an absolute importance, a seriousness and heaviness that in truth they do not have. When the world is not viewed from the perspective of the formless, it becomes a threatening place, and ultimately a place of despair. The Old Testament prophet must have felt this when he wrote, "All things are full of weariness. A man cannot utter it."[1]

## OBJECT CONSCIOUSNESS AND SPACE CONSCIOUSNESS

Most people's lives are cluttered up with things: material things, things to do, things to think about. Their lives are like the history of humanity, which Winston Churchill defined as "one damn thing after another." Their minds are filled up with the clutter of thoughts, one thought after another. This is the dimension of object consciousness that is many people's predominant reality, and that is why their lives are so out of balance. Object consciousness needs to be balanced by space consciousness for sanity to return to our planet and for humanity to fulfill its destiny. The arising of space consciousness is the next stage in the evolution of humanity.

Space consciousness means that in addition to being conscious of things—which always comes down to sense perceptions, thoughts, and emotions—there is an under- current of awareness. Awareness implies that you are not only conscious of things (objects), but you are also con- scious of being conscious. If you can sense an alert inner stillness in the background while things happen in the foreground—that's it! This dimension is there in everyone, but most people are completely unaware of it. Sometimes I point to it by saying, "Can you feel your own Presence?"

Space consciousness represents not only freedom from ego, but also from dependency on the things of this world, from materialism and materiality. It is the spiritual dimen- sion which alone can give transcendent and true meaning to this world.

Whenever you are upset about an event, a person, or a situation, the real cause is not the event, person, or situation but a loss of true perspective that only space can provide. You are trapped in object consciousness, unaware of the timeless inner space of consciousness itself. The words *This, too, will pass* when used as a pointer can restore awareness of that dimension to you.

Another pointer to the truth in you is contained in the following statement: "I am never upset for the reason I think."[2]

## FALLING BELOW AND
## RISING ABOVE THOUGHT

When you are very tired, you may become more peaceful, more relaxed, than in your usual state. This is because thinking is subsiding, and so you can't remember your mind-made problematic self anymore. You are moving toward sleep. When you drink alcohol or take certain drugs (provided they don't trigger your pain-body), you may also feel more relaxed, more carefree, and perhaps more alive for a while. You may start singing and dancing, which since ancient times are expressions of the joy of life. Because you are less burdened by your mind, you can glimpse the joy of Being. Perhaps this is the reason alcohol is also called "spirit." But there is a high price to pay: unconsciousness. Instead of rising above thought, you have fallen below it. A few more drinks, and you will have regressed to the vegetable realm.

Space consciousness has little to do with being "spaced out." Both states are beyond thought. This they have in common. The fundamental difference, however, is that in the former, you rise above thought; in the latter, you fall below it. One is the next step in the evolution of human consciousness, the other a regression to a stage we left behind eons ago.

## TELEVISION

Watching television is the favorite leisure activity or rather nonactivity for millions of people around the world. The average American, by the time he is sixty years old, will have spent fifteen years staring at the TV screen. In many other countries the figures are similar.

Many people find watching TV "relaxing." Observe yourself closely and you will find that the longer the screen remains the focus of your attention, the more your thought activity becomes suspended, and for long periods you are watching the talk show, game show, sitcom, or even commercials with almost no thought being generated by your mind. Not only do you not remember your problems anymore, but you become temporarily free of yourself—and what could be more relaxing than that?

So does TV watching create inner space? Does it cause you to be present? Unfortunately, it does not. Although for long periods your mind may not be generating any thoughts, it has linked into the thought activity of the television show. It has linked up with the TV version of the collective mind, and is thinking its thoughts. Your mind is inactive only in the sense that it is not producing thoughts. It is, however, continuously absorbing thoughts and images that come through the TV screen. This induces a trancelike passive state of heightened susceptibility, not unlike hypnosis. That is why it lends itself to manipulation of "public opinion," as politicians and special-interest groups as well as advertisers know and will pay millions of dollars to catch you in that state of receptive unawareness. They want their thoughts to become your thoughts, and usually they succeed.

So when watching television, the tendency is for you to fall below thought, not rise above it. Television has this in common with alcohol and certain other drugs. While it provides some relief from your mind, you again pay a high price: loss of consciousness. Like those drugs, it too has a strong addictive quality. You reach for the remote control to switch off and instead find yourself going through all the channels. Half an hour or an hour later, you are still watching, still going through the channels. The off button is the only one your finger seems unable to press. You are still watching, usually not because anything of interest has caught your attention, but precisely because there is nothing of interest to watch. Once you are hooked, the more trivial, the more meaningless, it is, the more addictive it becomes. If it were interesting, thought provoking, it would stimulate your mind into thinking for itself again, which is more conscious and therefore preferable to a TV-induced trance. Your attention would, therefore, no longer be totally held captive by the images on the screen.

The content of the program, if there is a certain quality to it, can to some extent counteract and sometimes even undo the hypnotic, mind-numbing effect of the medium of

TV. There are some programs that have been extremely helpful to many people; have changed their lives for the better, opened their heart, made them more conscious. Even some comedy shows, although they may be about nothing in particular, can be unintentionally spiritual by showing a caricature version of human folly and the ego. They teach us not to take anything too seriously, to approach life in a lighthearted way, and above all, they teach by making us laugh. Laughter is extraordinarily liberating as well as healing. Most of television, however, is as yet controlled by people who are totally controlled by the ego, and so the TV's hidden agenda becomes control of you by putting you to sleep, that is to say, making you unconscious. Yet there is enormous and still largely unexplored potential in the medium of television.

Avoid watching programs and commercials that assault you with a rapid succession of images that change every two or three seconds or less. Excessive TV watching and those programs in particular are largely responsible for attention deficit disorder, a mental dysfunction now affecting millions of children worldwide. A short attention span makes all your perceptions and relationships shallow and unsatisfying. Whatever you do, whatever action you perform in that state, lacks quality, because quality requires attention.

Frequent and prolonged TV watching not only makes you unconscious, it also induces passivity and drains you of energy. Therefore, rather than watching at random, choose the programs you want to see. Whenever you remember to do so, feel the aliveness inside your body as you watch. Alternatively, be aware of your breathing from time to time. Look away from the screen at regular intervals so that it does not completely take possession of your visual sense. Don't turn up the volume any higher than necessary so that the TV doesn't overwhelm you on the auditory level. Use the mute button during commercials. Make sure you don't go to sleep immediately after switching off the set or, even worse, fall asleep with the set still on.

## RECOGNIZING INNER SPACE

Space between thoughts is probably already arising sporadically in your life, and you may not even know it. A consciousness mesmerized by experiences and conditioned to identify exclusively with form, that is to say, object consciousness, finds it at first almost impossible to become aware of space. This ultimately means that you cannot become aware of yourself, because you are always aware of something else. You are continuously distracted by form. Even when you seem to be aware of yourself, you have made yourself into an object, a thought form, and so what you are aware of is a thought, not yourself.

When you hear of inner space, you may start seeking it, and, because you are seeking it as if you were looking for an object or for an experience, you cannot find it. This is the dilemma of all those who are seeking spiritual realization or enlightenment. Hence, Jesus said, "The kingdom of God is not coming with signs to be observed; nor will they say, 'Lo, here it is!' or 'There!' for behold, the kingdom of God is in the midst of you."[3]

If you are not spending all of your waking life in discontent, worry, anxiety, depression, despair, or consumed by other negative states; if you are able to enjoy simple things like listening to the sound of the rain or the wind; if you can see the beauty of clouds moving across the sky or be alone at times without feeling lonely or needing the mental stimulus of entertainment; if you find yourself treating a complete stranger with heartfelt kindness without wanting anything from him or her . . . it means that a space has opened up, no matter how briefly, in the otherwise incessant stream of thinking that is the human mind. When this happens, there is a sense of well-being, of alive peace, even though it may be subtle. The intensity will vary from a perhaps barely noticeable background sense of contentment to what the ancient sages of India called *ananda*—the bliss of Being. Because you have been conditioned to pay attention only to form, you are probably not aware of it except indirectly. For example, there is a common element in the ability to see beauty, to appreciate simple things, to enjoy your own company, or to relate to other people with loving kindness. This common element is a sense of contentment, peace, and aliveness that is the invisible background without which these experiences would not be possible.

Whenever there is beauty, kindness, the recognition of the goodness of simple things in your life, look for the background to that experience within yourself. But don't look for it as if you were looking for something. You cannot pin it down and say, "Now I have it," or grasp it mentally and define it in some way. It is like the cloudless sky. It has no form. It is space; it is stillness, the sweetness of Being and infinitely more than these words, which are only pointers. When you are able to sense it directly within yourself, it deepens. So when you appreciate something simple— a sound, a sight, a touch—when you see beauty, when you feel loving kindness toward another, sense the inner spaciousness that is the source and background to that experience.

Many poets and sages throughout the ages have observed that true happiness—I call it the joy of Being—is found in simple, seemingly unremarkable things. Most people, in their restless search for something significant to happen to them, continuously miss the insignificant, which may not be insignificant at all. The philosopher Nietzsche, in a rare moment of deep stillness, wrote, "For happiness, how little suffices for happiness! . . . the least thing precisely, the gentlest thing, the lightest thing, a lizard's rustling, a breath, a wisk, an eye glance—little maketh up the best happiness. Be still."[4]

Why is it the "least thing" that makes up "the best happiness"? Because true happiness is not *caused* by the thing or event, although this is how it first appears. The thing or event is so subtle, so unobtrusive, that it takes up only a small part of your consciousness—and the rest is inner space, consciousness itself unobstructed by form. Inner space consciousness and who you are in your essence are one and the same. In other words, the form of little things leaves room for inner space. And it is from inner space, the unconditioned consciousness itself, that true happiness, the joy of Being, emanates. To be aware of little, quiet things, however, you need to be quiet inside. A high degree of alertness is required. Be still. Look. Listen. Be present.

Here is another way of finding inner space: Become conscious of being conscious. Say or think "I Am" and add nothing to it. Be aware of the stillness that follows the I Am. Sense your presence, the naked, unveiled, unclothed beingness. It is untouched by young or old, rich or poor, good or bad, or any other attributes. It is the spacious womb of all creation, all form.

## CAN YOU HEAR THE MOUNTAIN STREAM?

A Zen Master was walking in silence with one of his disciples along a mountain trail. When they came to an ancient cedar tree, they sat down under it for a simple meal of some rice and vegetables. After the meal, the disciple, a young monk who had not yet found the key to the mystery of Zen, broke the silence by asking the Master, "Master, how do I enter Zen?"

He was, of course, inquiring how to enter the state of consciousness which is Zen.

The Master remained silent. Almost five minutes passed while the disciple anxiously waited for an answer. He was about to ask another question when the Master suddenly spoke. "Do you hear the sound of that mountain stream?"

The disciple had not been aware of any mountain stream. He had been too busy thinking about the meaning of Zen. Now, as he began to listen for the sound, his noisy mind subsided. At first he heard nothing. Then, his thinking gave way to heightened alertness, and suddenly he did hear the hardly perceptible murmur of a small stream in the far distance.

"Yes, I can hear it now," he said.

The Master raised his finger and, with a look in his eyes that in some way was both fierce and gentle, said, "Enter Zen from there."

The disciple was stunned. It was his first satori—a flash of enlightenment. He knew what Zen was without knowing what it was that he knew!

They continued on their journey in silence. The disciple was amazed at the aliveness of the world around him. He experienced everything as if for the first time. Gradually, however, he started thinking again. The alert stillness became covered up again by mental noise, and before long he had another question. "Master," he said, "I have been thinking. What would you have said if I hadn't been able to hear the mountain stream?" The Master stopped, looked at him, raised his finger and said, "Enter Zen from there."

## RIGHT ACTION

The ego asks, How can I make this situation fulfill my needs or how can I get to some other situation that *will* fulfill my needs?

Presence is a state of inner spaciousness. When you are present, you ask: How do I respond to the needs of this situation, of this moment? In fact, you don't even need to ask the question. You are still, alert, open to what *is*. You bring a new dimension into the situation: space. Then you look and you listen. Thus you become one with the situation. When instead of reacting against a situation, you merge with it, the solution arises out of the situation itself. Actually, it is not you, the person, who is looking and listening, but the alert stillness itself. Then, if action is possible or necessary, you take action or rather right action happens through you. Right action is action that is appropriate to the whole. When the action is accomplished, the alert, spacious stillness remains. There is nobody who raises his arms in a gesture of triumph shouting a defiant "Yeah!" There is no one who says, "Look, I did that."

All creativity comes out of inner spaciousness. Once the creation has happened and something has come into form, you have to be vigilant so that the notion of "me" or "mine" does not arise. If you take credit for what you accomplished, the ego has returned, and the spaciousness has become obscured.

## PERCEIVING WITHOUT NAMING

Most people are only peripherally aware of the world that surrounds them, especially if their surroundings are familiar. The voice in the head absorbs the greater part of their attention. Some people feel more alive when they travel and visit unfamiliar places or foreign countries because at those times sense perception—experiencing—takes up more of their consciousness than thinking. They become more present. Others remain completely possessed by the voice in the head even then. Their perceptions and experiences are distorted by instant judgments. They haven't really gone anywhere. Only their body is traveling, while they remain where they have always been: in their head.

This is most people's reality: As soon as something is perceived, it is named, interpreted, compared with something else, liked, disliked, or called good or bad by the phantom self, the ego. They are imprisoned in thought forms, in object consciousness.

You do not awaken spiritually until the compulsive and unconscious naming ceases, or at least you become aware of it and thus are able to observe it as it happens. It is through this constant naming that the ego remains in place as the unobserved mind. Whenever it ceases and even when you just become aware of it, there is inner space, and you are not possessed by the mind anymore.

Choose an object close to you—a pen, a chair, a cup, a plant—and explore it visually, that is to say, look at it with great interest, almost curiosity. Avoid any objects with strong personal associations that remind you of the past, such as where you bought it, who gave it to you, and so on. Also avoid anything that has writing on it such as a book or a bottle. It would stimulate thought. Without straining, relaxed but alert, give your complete attention to the object, every detail of it. If thoughts arise, don't get involved in them. It is not the thoughts you are interested in, but the act of perception itself. Can you take the thinking out of the perceiving? Can you look without the voice in your head commenting, drawing conclusions, comparing, or trying to figure something out? After a couple of minutes or so, let your gaze wander around the room or wherever you are, your alert attention lighting up each thing that it rests upon.

Then, listen to any sounds that may be present. Listen to

them in the same way as you looked at the things around you. Some sounds may be natural—water, wind, birds—while others are man-made. Some may be pleasant, others unpleasant. However, don't differentiate between good and bad. Allow each sound to be as it is, without interpretation. Here too, relaxed but alert attention is the key.

When you look and listen in this way, you may become aware of a subtle and at first perhaps hardly noticeable sense of calm. Some people feel it as a stillness in the background. Others call it peace. When consciousness is no longer totally absorbed by thinking, some of it remains in its formless, unconditioned, original state. This is inner space.

## WHO IS THE EXPERIENCER?

What you see and hear, taste, touch, and smell are, of course, sense objects. They are what you experience. But who is the subject, the experiencer? If you now say, for example, "Well, of course, I, Jane Smith, senior accountant, forty-five years old, divorced, mother of two, American, am the subject, the experiencer," you are mistaken. Jane Smith and whatever else becomes identified with the mental concept of Jane Smith are all objects of experience, not the experiencing subject.

Every experience has three possible ingredients: sense perceptions, thoughts or mental images, and emotions. Jane

Smith, senior accountant, forty-five years old, mother of two, divorced, American—these are all thoughts and therefore part of what you experience the moment you think these thoughts. They and whatever else you can say and think about yourself are objects, not the subject. They are experience, not the experiencer. You can add a thousand more definitions (thoughts) of who you are and by doing so will certainly increase the complexity of the experience of yourself (as well as your psychiatrist's income) but, in this way, you will not end up with the subject, the experiencer who is prior to all experience but without whom there would be no experience.

So who is the experiencer? You are. And who are you? Consciousness. And what is consciousness? This question cannot be answered. The moment you answer it, you have falsified it, made it into another object. Consciousness, the traditional word for which is *spirit,* cannot be known in the normal sense of the word, and seeking it is futile. All knowing is within the realm of duality—subject and object, the knower and the known. The subject, the I, the knower without which nothing could be known, perceived, thought, or felt, must remain forever unknowable. This is because the I has no form. Only forms can be known, and yet without the formless dimension, the world of form could not be. It is the luminous space in which the world arises and subsides. That space is the life that I Am. It is timeless. I Am timeless, eternal. What happens in that space is relative and temporary: pleasure and pain, gain and loss, birth and death.

The greatest impediment to the discovery of inner space, the greatest impediment to finding the experiencer, is to become so enthralled by the experience that you lose yourself in it. It means consciousness is lost in its own dream. You get taken in by every thought, every emotion, and every experience to such a degree that you are in fact in a dreamlike state. This has been the normal state of humanity for thousands of years.

Although you cannot know consciousness, you can become conscious of it as yourself. You can sense it directly in any situation, no matter where you are. You can sense it here and now as your very Presence, the inner space in which the words on this page are perceived and become thoughts. It is the underlying I Am. The words you are reading and thinking are the foreground, and the I Am is the substratum, the underlying background to every experience, thought, feeling.

## THE BREATH

Discover inner space by creating gaps in the stream of thinking. Without those gaps, your thinking becomes repetitive, uninspired, devoid of any creative spark, which is how it still is for most people on the planet. You don't need to be concerned with the duration of those gaps. A few seconds is good enough. Gradually, they will lengthen by themselves, without any effort on your part. More important than their length is to bring them in frequently so that your daily activities and your stream of thinking become interspersed with space.

Someone recently showed me the annual prospectus of a large spiritual organization. When I looked through it, I was impressed by the wide choice of interesting seminars and workshops. It reminded me of a smorgasbord, one of those Scandinavian buffets where you can take your pick from a huge variety of enticing dishes. The person asked me whether I could recommend one or two courses. "I don't know," I said. "They all look so interesting. But I do know this," I added. "Be aware of your breathing as often as you are able, whenever you remember. Do that for one year, and it will be more powerfully transformative than attending all of these courses. And it's free."

Being aware of your breathing takes attention away from thinking and creates space. It is one way of generating consciousness. Although the fullness of consciousness is already there as the unmanifested, we are here to bring consciousness into this dimension.

Be aware of your breathing. Notice the sensation of the breath. Feel the air moving in and out of your body. Notice how the chest and abdomen expand and contract slightly with the in- and outbreath. One conscious breath is enough to make some space where before there was the uninterrupted succession of one thought after another. One conscious breath (two or three would be even better), taken many times a day, is an excellent way of bringing space into your life. Even if you meditated on your breathing for two hours or more, which some people do, one breath is all you ever need to be aware of, indeed ever can be aware of. The rest is memory or anticipation, which is to say, thought. Breathing isn't really something that you do but something that you witness as it happens. Breathing happens by itself. The intelligence within the body is doing it. All you have to do is watch it happening. There is no strain or effort involved. Also, notice the brief cessation of the breath, particularly the still point at the end of the out-breath, before you start breathing in again.

Many people's breath is unnaturally shallow. The more you are aware of the breath, the more its natural depth will reestablish itself.

Because breath has no form as such, it has since ancient times been equated with spirit—the formless one Life. "God formed man of dust from the ground and breathed into his nostrils the breath of life and the man became a living creature."[5] The German word for breathing—*atmen*—is derived from the ancient Indian (Sanskrit) word *Atman*, meaning the indwelling divine spirit or God within.

The fact that breath has no form is one of the reasons why breath awareness is an extremely effective way of bringing space into your life, of generating consciousness.

It is an excellent meditation object precisely because it is not an object, has no shape or form. The other reason is that breath is one of the most subtle and seemingly insignificant phenomena, the "least thing" that according to Nietzsche makes up the "best happiness." Whether or not you practice breath awareness as an actual formal meditation is up to you. Formal meditation, however, is no substitute for bringing space consciousness into everyday life.

Being aware of your breath forces you into the present moment—the key to all inner transformation. Whenever you are conscious of the breath, you are absolutely present. You may also notice that you cannot think *and* be aware of your breathing. Conscious breathing stops your mind. But far from being in a trance or half asleep, you are fully awake and highly alert. You are not falling below thinking, but rising above it. And if you look more closely, you will find that those two things—coming fully into the present moment and ceasing thinking without loss of consciousness—are actually one and the same: the arising of space consciousness.

## ADDICTIONS

A long-standing compulsive behavior pattern may be called an addiction, and an addiction lives inside you as a quasi-entity or subpersonality, an energy field that periodically takes you over completely. It even takes over your mind, the voice in your head, which then becomes the voice of the addiction. It may be saying, "You've had a rough day. You deserve a treat. Why deny yourself the only pleasure that is left in your life?" And so, if you are identified with the internal voice due to lack of awareness, you find yourself walking to the fridge and reaching for that rich chocolate cake. At other times, the addiction may bypass the thinking mind completely and you suddenly find yourself puffing on a cigarette or holding a drink. "How did that get into my hand?" Taking the cigarette out of the packet and lighting it, or pouring yourself a drink were actions performed in complete unconsciousness.

If you have a compulsive behavior pattern such as smoking, overeating, drinking, TV watching, Internet addiction, or whatever it may be, this is what you can do: When you notice the compulsive need arising in you, stop and take three conscious breaths. This generates awareness. Then for a few minutes be aware of the compulsive urge itself as an energy field inside you. Consciously feel that need to physically or mentally ingest or consume a certain substance or the desire to act out some form of compulsive behavior. Then take a few more conscious breaths. After that you may find that the compulsive urge has disappeared—for the time being. Or you may find that it still overpowers you, and you cannot help but indulge or act it out again. Don't make it into a problem. Make the addiction part of your awareness practice in the way described above. As awareness grows, addictive patterns will weaken and eventually dissolve. Remember, however, to catch any thoughts that justify the addictive behavior, sometimes with clever arguments, as they arise in your mind. Ask yourself, Who is talking here? And you will realize the addiction is talking. As long as you know that, as long as you are present as the observer of your mind, it is less likely to trick you into doing what it wants.

## INNER BODY AWARENESS

Another simple but highly effective way of finding space in your life is closely linked to the breath. You will find that by feeling the subtle flow of air in and out of the body as well as the rise and fall of your chest and abdomen, you are also becoming aware of the inner body. Your attention may then shift from the breath to that felt aliveness within you, diffused throughout the body.

Most people are so distracted by their thoughts, so identified with the voices in their heads, they can no longer feel the aliveness within them. To be unable to feel the life that animates the physical body, the very life that you are, is the greatest deprivation that can happen to you. You then begin to look not only for substitutes for that natural state of well-being within, but also for something to cover up the continuous unease that you feel when you are not in touch with the aliveness that is always there but usually overlooked. Some of the substitutes people seek out are drug-induced highs, sensory overstimulation such as excessively loud music, thrills or dangerous activities, or an obsession with sex. Even drama in relationships is used as a substitute for that genuine sense of aliveness. The most sought-after cover-up for the continuous background unease are intimate relationships: a man or a woman who is going to "make me happy." It is, of course, also one of the most frequently experienced of all the "letdowns." And when the unease surfaces again, people will usually blame their partner for it.

Take two or three conscious breaths. Now see if you can detect a subtle sense of aliveness that pervades your entire inner body. Can you feel your body from within, so to speak? Sense briefly specific parts of your body. Feel your hands, then your arms, feet, and legs. Can you feel your abdomen, chest, neck, and head? What about your lips? Is there life in them? Then become aware again of the inner body as a whole. You may want to close your eyes initially for this practice, and once you can feel your body, open your eyes, look around, and continue to feel your body at the same time. Some readers may find there is no need to close their eyes; they can in fact feel their inner body as they read this.

## INNER AND OUTER SPACE

Your inner body is not solid but spacious. It is not your physical form but the life that animates the physical form. It is the intelligence that created and sustains the body, simultaneously coordinating hundreds of different functions of such extraordinary complexity that the human mind can only understand a tiny fraction of it. When you become aware of it, what is really happening is that the intelligence is becoming aware of itself. It is the elusive "life" that no scientist has ever found because the consciousness that is looking for it *is it*.

Physicists have discovered that the apparent solidity of matter is an illusion created by our senses. This includes the physical body, which we perceive and think of as form, but 99.99 % of which is actually empty space. This is how vast the space is between the atoms compared to their size, and there is as much space again within each atom. The physical body is no more than a misperception of who you are. In many ways, it is a microcosmic version of outer space. To give you an idea of how vast the space is between celestial bodies, consider this: Light traveling at a constant speed of 186,000 miles (300,000 kilometers) per second takes just over one second to travel between the earth and the moon; light from the sun takes about eight minutes to reach the earth. Light from our nearest neighbor in space, a star called Proxima Centauri, which is the sun that is closest to our own sun, travels for 4.5 years before it reaches the earth. This is how vast the space is that surrounds us. And then there is the intergalactic space, whose vastness defies all comprehension. Light from the galaxy closest to our own, the Andromeda Galaxy, takes 2.4 million years to reach us. Isn't it amazing that your body is just as spacious as the universe?

So your physical body, which is form, reveals itself as essentially formless when you go deeper into it. It becomes a doorway into inner space. Although inner space has no form, it is intensely alive. That "empty space" is life in its fullness, the unmanifested Source out of which all manifestation flows. The traditional word for that Source is God.

Thoughts and words belong to the world of form; they cannot express the formless. So when you say, "I can feel my inner body" that is a misperception created by thought. What is really happening is that the consciousness that appears as the body—the consciousness that I Am—is becoming conscious of itself. When I no longer confuse who I am with a temporary form of "me," then the dimension of the limitless and the eternal—God—can express itself through "me" and guide "me." It also frees me from dependency on form. However, a purely intellectual recognition or belief that "I am not this form" does not help. The all-important question is: At this moment, can I sense the presence of inner space, which really means, can I sense my own Presence, or rather, the Presence that I Am?

Or we can approach this truth using a different pointer. Ask yourself, "Am I aware not only of what is happening at this moment, but also of the Now itself as the living time- less inner space in which everything happens?" Although this question seems to have nothing to do with the inner body, you may be surprised that by becoming aware of the space of Now, you suddenly feel more alive inside. You are feeling the aliveness of the inner body—the aliveness that is an intrinsic part of the joy of Being. We have to enter the body to go beyond it and find out that we are not that.

As much as possible in everyday life, use awareness of the inner body to create space. When waiting, when listening to someone, when pausing to look at the sky, a tree, a flower, your partner, or child, feel the aliveness within at the same time. This means part of your attention or con- sciousness remains formless, and the rest is available for the outer world of form. Whenever you "inhabit" your body in this way, it serves as an anchor for staying present in the Now. It prevents you from losing yourself in thinking, in emotions, or in external situations.

When you think, feel, perceive, and experience, con- sciousness is born into form. It is reincarnating—into a thought, a feeling, a sense perception, an experience. The cycle of rebirths that Buddhists hope to get out of even- tually is happening continuously, and it is only at this moment—through the power of Now—that you can get out of it. Through complete acceptance of the form of the

Now, you become internally aligned with space, which is the essence of Now. Through acceptance, you become spacious inside. Aligned with space instead of form: That brings true perspective and balance into your life.

## NOTICING THE GAPS

Throughout the day, there is a continuously changing succession of things that you see and hear. In the first moment of seeing something or hearing a sound—and more so if it is unfamiliar—before the mind names or interprets what you see or hear, there is usually a gap of alert attention in which the perception occurs. That is the inner space. Its duration differs from person to person. It is easy to miss because in many people those spaces are extremely short, perhaps only a second or less.

This is what happens: A new sight or sound arises, and in the first moment of perception, there is a brief cessation in the habitual stream of thinking. Consciousness is diverted away from thought because it is required for sense perception. A very unusual sight or sound may leave you "speechless"— even inside, that is to say, bring about a longer gap.

The frequency and duration of those spaces determine your ability to enjoy life, to feel an inner connectedness with other human beings as well as nature. It also determines the degree to which you are free of ego because ego implies complete unawareness of the dimension of space.

When you become conscious of these brief spaces as they happen naturally, they will lengthen, and as they do, you will experience with increasing frequency the joy of perceiving with little or no interference of thinking. The world around you then feels fresh, new, and alive. The more you perceive life through a mental screen of abstraction and conceptualization, the more lifeless and flat the world around you becomes.

## LOSE YOURSELF TO FIND YOURSELF

Inner space also arises whenever you let go of the need to emphasize your form-identity. That need is of the ego. It is not a true need. We have already touched briefly upon this. Whenever you relinquish one of these behavior patterns, inner space emerges. You become more truly yourself. To the ego it will seem as if you were losing yourself, but the opposite is the case. Jesus already taught that you need to lose yourself to find yourself. Whenever you let go of one of these patterns, you de-emphasize who you are on the level of form and who you are beyond form emerges more fully. You become less, so you can be more.

Here are some ways in which people unconsciously try to emphasize their form-identity. If you are alert enough, you may be able to detect some of these unconscious patterns within yourself: demanding recognition for something you did and getting angry or upset if you don't get it;

trying to get attention by talking about your problems, the story of your illnesses, or making a scene; giving your opinion when nobody has asked for it and it makes no difference to the situation; being more concerned with how the other person sees you than with the other person, which is to say, using other people for egoic reflection or as ego enhancers; trying to make an impression on others through possessions, knowledge, good looks, status, physical strength, and so on; bringing about temporary ego inflation through angry reaction against something or someone; taking things personally, feeling offended; making yourself right and others wrong through futile mental or verbal complaining; wanting to be seen, or to appear important.

Once you have detected such a pattern within yourself, I suggest that you conduct an experiment. Find out what it feels like and what happens if you let go of that pattern. Just drop it and see what happens.

De-emphasizing who you are on the level of form is another way of generating consciousness. Discover the enormous power that flows through you into the world when you stop emphasizing your form-identity.


## STILLNESS

It has been said: "Stillness is the language God speaks, and everything else is a bad translation." Stillness is really another word for space. Becoming conscious of stillness whenever we encounter it in our lives will connect us with the formless and timeless dimension within ourselves, that which is beyond thought, beyond ego. It may be the stillness that pervades the world of nature, or the stillness in your room in the early hours of the morning, or the silent gaps in between sounds. Stillness has no form—that is why through thinking we cannot become aware of it. Thought is form. Being aware of stillness means to be still. To be still is to be conscious without thought. You are never more essentially, more deeply, yourself than when you are still. When you are still, you are who you were before you temporarily assumed this physical and mental form called a person. You are also who you will be when the form dissolves. When you are still, you are who you are beyond your temporal existence: consciousness—unconditioned, formless, eternal.

## CHAPTER NINE

# Your Inner Purpose

As soon as you rise above mere survival, the question of meaning and purpose becomes of paramount importance in your life. Many people feel caught up in the routines of daily living that seem to deprive their life of significance. Some believe life is passing them by or has passed them by already. Others feel severely restricted by the demands of their job and supporting a family or by their financial or living situation. Some are consumed by acute stress, others by acute boredom. Some are lost in frantic doing; others are lost in stagnation. Many people long for the freedom and expansion that prosperity promises. Others already enjoy the relative freedom that comes with prosperity and discover that even that is not enough to endow their lives with meaning. There is no substitute for finding true purpose.

But the true or primary purpose of your life cannot be found on the outer level. It does not concern what you do but what you are—that is to say, your state of consciousness.

So the most important thing to realize is this: Your life has an inner purpose and an outer purpose. Inner purpose concerns Being and is primary. Outer purpose concerns doing and is secondary. While this book speaks mainly of your inner purpose, this chapter and the next will also address the question of how to align outer purpose and inner purpose in your life. Inner and outer, however, are so intertwined that it is almost impossible to speak of one without referring to the other.

Your inner purpose is to awaken. It is as simple as that. You share that purpose with every other person on the planet—because it is the purpose of humanity. Your inner purpose is an essential part of the purpose of the whole, the universe and its emerging intelligence. Your outer purpose can change over time. It varies greatly from person to person. Finding and living in alignment with the inner purpose is the foundation for fulfilling your outer purpose. It is the basis for true success. Without that alignment, you can still achieve certain things through effort, struggle, determination, and sheer hard work or cunning. But there is no joy in such endeavor, and it invariably ends in some form of suffering.

## AWAKENING

Awakening is a shift in consciousness in which thinking and awareness separate. For most people it is not an event but a process they undergo. Even those rare beings who experience a sudden, dramatic, and seemingly irreversible awakening will still go through a process in which the new state of consciousness gradually flows into and transforms everything they do and so becomes integrated into their lives.

Instead of being lost in your thinking, when you are awake you recognize yourself as the awareness behind it. Thinking then ceases to be a self-serving autonomous activity that takes possession of you and runs your life. Awareness takes over from thinking. Instead of being in charge of your life, thinking becomes the servant of awareness. Awareness is conscious connection with universal intelligence. Another word for it is Presence: consciousness without thought.

The initiation of the awakening process is an act of grace. You cannot make it happen nor can you prepare yourself for it or accumulate credits toward it. There isn't a tidy sequence of logical steps that leads toward it, although the mind would love that. You don't have to become worthy first. It may come to the sinner before it comes to the saint, but not necessarily. That's why Jesus associated with all kinds of people, not just the respectable ones. There is nothing you can do about awakening. Whatever you do will be the ego trying to add awakening or enlightenment to itself as its most prized possession and thereby making itself more important and bigger. Instead of awakening, you add the *concept* of awakening to your mind, or the mental image of what an awakened or enlightened person is like, and then try to live up to that image. Living up to an image that you have of yourself or that other people have of you is inauthentic living—another unconscious role the ego plays.

So if there is nothing you can do about awakening, if it has either already happened or not yet happened, how can it be the primary purpose of your life? Does not purpose imply that you can do something about it?

Only the first awakening, the first glimpse of consciousness without thought, happens by grace, without any doing on your part. If you find this book incomprehensible or meaningless, it has not yet happened to you. If something within you responds to it, however, if you somehow recognize the truth in it, it means the process of awakening has begun. Once it has done so, it cannot be reversed, although it can be delayed by the ego. For some people, the reading of this book will initiate the awakening process. For others, the function of this book is to help them recognize that they have already begun to awaken and to intensify and accelerate the process. Another function of this book is to help people recognize the ego within them whenever it tries to regain control and obscure the arising awareness.

For some, the awakening happens as they suddenly become aware of the kinds of thoughts they habitually think, especially persistent negative thoughts that they may have been identified with all of their lives. Suddenly there is an awareness that is aware of thought but is not part of it.

What is the relationship between awareness and thinking? Awareness is the space in which thoughts exist when that space has become conscious of itself.

Once you have had a glimpse of awareness or Presence, you know it firsthand. It is no longer just a concept in your mind. You can then make a conscious choice to be present rather than to indulge in useless thinking. You can invite Presence into your life, that is to say, make space. With the grace of awakening comes responsibility. You can either try to go on as if nothing has happened, or you can see its significance and recognize the arising of awareness as the most important thing that *can* happen to you. Opening yourself to the emerging consciousness and bringing its light into this world then becomes the primary purpose of your life.

"I want to know the mind of God," Einstein said. "The rest are details." What is the mind of God? Consciousness. What does it mean to know the mind of God? To be aware. What are the details? Your outer purpose, and whatever happens outwardly.

So while you are perhaps still waiting for something significant to happen in your life, you may not realize that the most significant thing that can happen to a human being has already happened within you: the beginning of the separation process of thinking and awareness.

Many people who are going through the early stages of the awakening process are no longer certain what their outer purpose is. What drives the world no longer drives them. Seeing the madness of our civilization so clearly, they may feel somewhat alienated from the culture around them. Some feel that they inhabit a no-man's-land between two worlds. They are no longer run by the ego, yet the arising awareness has not yet become fully integrated into their lives. Inner and outer purpose have not merged.

## A DIALOGUE ON INNER PURPOSE

The following dialogue condenses numerous conversations I have had with people who were looking for their true life purpose. Something is true when it resonates with and expresses your innermost Being, when it is in alignment with your inner purpose. This is why I am directing their attention to their inner and primary purpose first.

*I don't know exactly what it is, but I want some change in my life. I want expansion; I want to be doing something meaningful and, yes, I want prosperity and the freedom that comes with it. I want to do something significant, something that makes a difference in the world. But if you asked me what exactly I want, I would have to say that I don't know. Can you help me find my life purpose?*

Your purpose is to sit here and talk to me, because that's where you are and that's what you are doing. Until you get up and do something else. Then, that becomes your purpose.

*So my purpose is to sit in my office for the next thirty years until I retire or get laid off?*

You are not in your office now, so that's not your purpose. When you do sit in your office and do whatever you do, then that is your purpose. Not for the next thirty years, but for now.

*I think there is some misunderstanding here. For you, purpose means what you are doing now; for me it means having an overall aim in life, something big and significant that gives meaning to what I do, something that makes a difference. Shuffling papers in the office is not it. I know that.*

As long as you are unaware of Being, you will seek meaning only within the dimension of doing and of future, that is to say, the dimension of time. And whatever meaning or fulfillment you find will dissolve or turn out to have been a deception. Invariably, it will be destroyed by time. Any meaning we find on that level is true only relatively and temporarily.

For example, if caring for your children gives meaning to your life, what happens to that meaning when they don't need you and perhaps don't even listen to you anymore? If helping others gives meaning to your life, you depend on others being worse off than yourself so that your life can continue to be meaningful and you can feel good about yourself. If the desire to excel, win, or succeed at this or that activity provides you with meaning, what if you never win or your winning streak comes to an end one day, as it will? You would then have to look to your imagination or memories—a very unsatisfactory place to bring some meager meaning into your life. "Making it" in whatever field is only meaningful as long as there are thousands or millions of others who don't make it, so you need other human beings to "fail" so that your life can have meaning.

I am not saying here that helping others, caring for your children, or striving for excellence in whatever field are not worthwhile things to do. For many people, they are an important part of their outer purpose, but outer purpose alone is always relative, unstable, and impermanent. This does not mean that you should not be engaged in those activities. It means you should connect them to your inner, primary purpose, so that a deeper meaning flows into what you do.

Without living in alignment with your primary purpose, whatever purpose you come up with, even if it is to create heaven on earth, will be of the ego or become destroyed by time. Sooner or later, it will lead to suffering. If you ignore your inner purpose, no matter what you do, even if it looks spiritual, the ego will creep into *how* you do it, and so the means will corrupt the end. The common saying "The road to hell is paved with good intentions" points to this truth. In other words, not your aims or your actions are primary, but the state of consciousness out of which they come. Fulfilling your primary purpose is laying the foundation for a new reality, a new earth. Once that foundation is there, your external purpose becomes charged with spiritual power because your aims and intentions will be one with the evolutionary impulse of the universe.

The separation of thinking and awareness, which lies at the core of your primary purpose, happens through the negation of time. We are not speaking here, of course, of the use of time for practical purposes, such as making an appointment or planning a trip. We are not speaking of clock time, but of psychological time, which is the mind's deep-seated habit of seeking the fullness of life in the future where it cannot be found and ignoring the only point of access to it: the present moment.

When you look upon what you do or where you are as the main purpose of your life, you negate time. This is enormously empowering. The negation of time in what you do also provides the link between your inner and outer purposes, between Being and doing. When you negate time, you negate the ego. Whatever you do, you will be doing extraordinarily well, because the doing itself becomes the focal point of your attention. Your doing then becomes a channel through which consciousness enters this world. This means there is quality in what you do, even in the most simple action, like turning the pages in the phone book or walking across the room. The main purpose for turning the pages is to turn the pages; the secondary purpose is to find a phone number. The main purpose for walking across the room is to walk across the room; the secondary purpose is to pick up a book at the other end, and the moment you pick up the book, that becomes your main purpose.

You may remember the paradox of time we mentioned earlier: Whatever you do takes time, and yet it is always now. So while your inner purpose is to negate time, your outer purpose necessarily involves future and so could not exist without time. But it is always secondary. Whenever you become anxious or stressed, outer purpose has taken over, and you lost sight of your inner purpose. You have forgotten that your state of consciousness is primary, all else secondary.

*Would living like this not stop me from looking to achieve something great? My fear is that I will remain stuck with doing little things for the rest of my life, things that are of no consequence. I'm afraid of never rising above mediocrity, never daring to achieve anything great, not fulfilling my potential.*

The great arises out of small things that are honored and cared for. Everybody's life really consists of small things. Greatness is a mental abstraction and a favorite fantasy of the ego. The paradox is that the foundation for greatness is honoring the small things of the present moment instead of pursuing the idea of greatness. The present moment is always small in the sense that it is always simple, but concealed within it lies the greatest power. Like the atom, it is one of the smallest things yet contains enormous power. Only when you align yourself with the present moment do you have access to that power. Or it may be more true to say that *it* then has access to you and through you to this world. Jesus was referring to this power when he said, "It is not I but the Father within me who does the works." And "I can of my own self do nothing."[1] Anxiety, stress, and negativity cut you off from that power. The illusion that you are separate from the power that runs the universe returns. You feel yourself to be alone again, struggling against something or trying to achieve this or that. But why did anxiety, stress, or negativity arise? Because you turned away from the present moment. And why did you do that? You thought something else was more important. You forgot your main purpose. One small error, one misperception, creates a world of suffering.

Through the present moment, you have access to the power of life itself, that which has traditionally been called "God." As soon as you turn away from it, God ceases to be a reality in your life, and all you are left with is the mental *concept* of God, which some people believe in and others deny. Even belief in God is only a poor substitute for the living reality of God manifesting every moment of your life.

*Would complete harmony with the present moment not imply the cessation of all movement? Doesn't the existence of any goal imply that there is a temporary disruption in that harmony with the present moment and perhaps a reestablishment of harmony at a higher or more complex level once the goal has been attained? I imagine that the sapling that pushes its way through the soil can't be in total harmony with the present moment either because it has a goal: It wants to become a big tree. Maybe once it has reached maturity it will live in harmony with the present moment.*

The sapling doesn't want anything because it is at one with the totality, and the totality acts through it. "Look at the lilies of the field, how they grow" said Jesus, "they toil not, neither do they spin. Yet even Solomon in all his glory was not arrayed like one of these."[2] We could say that the totality—Life—*wants* the sapling to become a tree, but the sapling doesn't see itself as separate from life and so wants nothing for itself. It is one with what Life wants. That's why it isn't worried or stressed. And if it has to die prematurely, it dies with ease. It is as surrendered in death as it is in life. It senses, no matter how obscurely, its rootedness in Being, the formless and eternal one Life.

Like the Taoist sages of ancient China, Jesus likes to draw our attention to nature because he sees a power at work in it that humans have lost touch with. It is the creative power of the universe. Jesus goes on to say that if God clothes simple flowers in such beauty, how much more will God clothe you. That is to say, that while nature is a beautiful expression of the evolutionary impulse of the universe, when humans become aligned with the intelligence that underlies it, they will express that same impulse on a higher, more wondrous level.

So be true to life by being true to your inner purpose. As you become present and thereby total in what you do, your actions become charged with spiritual power. At first there may be no noticeable change in *what* you do—only the *how* changes. Your primary purpose is now to enable consciousness to flow into what you do. The secondary purpose is whatever you want to achieve through the doing. Whereas the notion of purpose before was always associated with future, there is now a deeper purpose that can only be found in the present, through the denial of time.

When you meet with people, at work or wherever it may be, give them your fullest attention. You are no longer there primarily as a person, but as a field of awareness, of alert Presence. The original reason for interacting with the other person—buying or selling something, requesting or giving information, and so on—now becomes secondary. The field of awareness that arises between you becomes the primary purpose for the interaction. That space of awareness becomes more important than what you may be talking about, more important than physical or thought objects. The human *Being* becomes more important than the things of this world. It does not mean you neglect whatever needs to be done on a practical level. In fact, the doing unfolds not only more easily, but more powerfully when the dimension of Being is acknowledged and so becomes primary. The arising of that unifying field of awareness between human beings is the most essential factor in relationships on the new earth.

*Is the notion of success just an egoic illusion? How do we measure true success?*

The world will tell you that success is achieving what you set out to do. It will tell you that success is winning, that finding recognition and/or prosperity are essential ingredients in any success. All or some of the above are usually by-products of success, but they are not success. The conventional notion of success is concerned with the outcome of what you do. Some say that success is the result of a combination of hard work and luck, or determination and talent, or being in the right place at the right time. While any of these may be determinants of success, they are not its essence. What the world doesn't tell you— because it doesn't know—is that you cannot *become* successful. You can only *be* successful. Don't let a mad world tell you that success is anything other than a successful present moment. And what is that? There is a sense of quality in what you do, even the most simple action. Quality implies care and attention, which come with awareness. Quality requires your Presence.

Let's say that you are a businessperson and after two years of intense stress and strain you finally manage to come out with a product or service that sells well and makes money. Success? In conventional terms, yes. In reality, you spent two years polluting your body as well as the earth with negative energy, made yourself and those around you miserable, and affected many others you never even met. The unconscious assumption behind all such action is that success is a future event, and that the end justifies the means. But the end and the means are one. And if the means did not contribute to human happiness, neither will the end. The outcome, which is inseparable from the actions that led to it, is already contaminated by those actions and so will create further unhappiness. This is karmic action, which is the unconscious perpetuation of unhappiness.

As you already know, your secondary or outer purpose lies within the dimension of time, while your main purpose is inseparable from the Now and therefore requires the negation of time. How are they reconciled? By realizing that your entire life journey ultimately consists of the step you are taking at this moment. There is always only this one step, and so you give it your fullest attention. This doesn't mean you don't know where you are going; it just means this step is primary, the destination secondary. And what you encounter at your destination once you get there depends on the quality of this one step. Another way of putting it: What the future holds for you depends on your state of consciousness now.

When doing becomes infused with the timeless quality

of Being, *that* is success. Unless Being flows into doing, un-less you are present, you lose yourself in whatever you do. You also lose yourself in thinking, as well as in your reac-tions to what happens externally.

*What exactly do you mean when you say, "You lose yourself"?*

The essence of who you are is consciousness. When consciousness (you) becomes completely identified with thinking and thus forgets its essential nature, it loses itself in thought. When it becomes identified with mental-emotional formations such as wanting and fearing—the primary motivating forces of the ego—it loses itself in those formations. Consciousness also loses itself when it identifies with acting and reacting to what happens. Every thought, every desire or fear, every action or reaction, is then infused with a false sense of self that is incapable of sensing the simple joy of Being and so seeks pleasure, and sometimes even pain, as substitutes for it. This is living in forgetful-ness of Being. In that state of forgetfulness of who you are, every success is no more than a passing delusion. What-ever you achieve, soon you will be unhappy again, or some new problem or dilemma will draw your attention in completely.

*How do I go from realizing what my inner purpose is to finding out what I am supposed to do on the outer level?*

The outer purpose varies greatly from person to person, and no outer purpose lasts forever. It is subject to time and then replaced by some other purpose. The extent to which dedication to the inner purpose of awakening changes the external circumstances of your life also varies greatly. For some people, there is a sudden or gradual break with their past: their work, living situation, relationships—everything undergoes profound change. Some of the change may be initiated by themselves, not through an agonizing decision-making process but by a sudden realization or recognition: This is what I have to do. The decision arrives ready-made, so to speak. It comes through awareness, not through thinking. You wake up one morning and you know what to do. Some people find themselves walking out of an insane work environment or living situation. So before you discover what is right for you on the external level, before you discover what works, what is compatible with the awakening consciousness, you may have to find out what is not right, what no longer works, what is incompatible with your inner purpose.

Other kinds of change may suddenly come to you from without. A chance meeting brings new opportunity and expansion into your life. A long-standing obstacle or conflict dissolves. Your friends either go through this inner transformation with you or drift out of your life. Some relationships dissolve, others deepen. You may get laid off from your job, or you become an agent for positive change at your workplace. Your spouse leaves you, or you reach a new level of intimacy. Some changes may look negative on the surface but you will soon realize that space is being created in your life for something new to emerge.

There may be a period of insecurity and uncertainty. What should I do? As the ego is no longer running your life, the psychological need for external security, which is illusory anyway, lessens. You are able to live with uncertainty, even enjoy it. When you become comfortable with uncertainty, infinite possibilities open up in your life. It means fear is no longer a dominant factor in what you do and no longer prevents you from taking action to initiate change. The Roman philosopher Tacitus rightly observed that "the desire for safety stands against every great and noble enterprise." If uncertainty is unacceptable to you, it turns into fear. If it is perfectly acceptable, it turns into increased aliveness, alertness, and creativity.

Many years ago, as a result of a strong inner impulse, I walked out of an academic career that the world would have called "promising," stepping into complete uncertainty; and out of that, after several years, emerged my new incarnation as a spiritual teacher. Much later, something similar happened again. The impulse came to give up my home in England and move to the West Coast of North America. I obeyed that impulse, although I didn't know the reason for it. Out of that move into uncertainty came *The Power of Now*, most of which was written in California and British Columbia while I didn't have a home of my own. I had virtually no income and lived on my savings, which were quickly running out. In fact, everything fell into place beautifully. I ran out of money just when I was getting close to finishing writing. I bought a lottery ticket and won $1,000, which kept me going for another month.

Not everybody, however, will have to go through drastic change in their external circumstances. At the other end of the spectrum you have people who stay exactly where they are and keep doing whatever they are doing. For them, only the *how* changes, not the *what*. This is not due to fear or inertia. What they are doing already is a perfect vehicle for consciousness to come into this world, and it needs no other. They too bring into manifestation the new earth.

*Shouldn't this be the case for everybody? If fulfilling your inner purpose is being at one with the present moment, why should anybody feel the need to remove themselves from their current work or living situation?*

Being at one with what *is* doesn't mean you no longer initiate change or become incapable of taking action. But the motivation to take action comes from a deeper level, not from egoic wanting or fearing. Inner alignment with the present moment opens your consciousness and brings it into alignment with the whole, of which the present moment is an integral part. The whole, the totality of life, then acts through you.

*What do you mean by the whole?*

On the one hand, the whole comprises all that exists. It

is the world or the cosmos. But all things in existence, from microbes to human beings to galaxies, are not really separate things or entities, but form part of a web of interconnected multidimensional processes.

There are two reasons why we don't see this unity, why we see things as separate. One is perception, which reduces reality to what is accessible to us through the small range of our senses: what we can see, hear, smell, taste, and touch. But when we perceive without interpreting or mental labeling, which means without adding thought to our perceptions, we can actually still sense the deeper connectedness underneath our perception of seemingly separate things.

The other more serious reason for the illusion of separateness is compulsive thinking. It is when we are trapped in incessant streams of compulsive thinking that the universe really disintegrates for us, and we lose the ability to sense the interconnectedness of all that exists. Thinking cuts reality up into lifeless fragments. Extremely unintelligent and destructive action arises out of such a fragmented view of reality.

However, there is an even deeper level to the whole than the interconnectedness of everything in existence. At that deeper level, all things are one. It is the Source, the unmanifested one Life. It is the timeless intelligence that manifests as a universe unfolding in time.

The whole is made up of existence and Being, the manifested and the unmanifested, the world and God. So when you become aligned with the whole, you become a conscious part of the interconnectedness of the whole and its purpose: the emergence of consciousness into this world. As a result, spontaneous helpful occurrences, chance encounters, coincidences, and synchronistic events happen much more frequently. Carl Jung called synchronicity an "acausal connecting principle." This means there is no causal connection between synchronistic events on our surface level of reality. It is an outer manifestation of an underlying intelligence behind the world of appearances and a deeper connectedness that our mind cannot understand. But we can be conscious participants in the unfolding of that intelligence, the flowering consciousness.

Nature exists in a state of unconscious oneness with the whole. This, for example, is why virtually no wild animals were killed in the tsunami disaster of 2004. Being more in touch with the totality than humans, they could sense the tsunami's approach long before it could be seen or heard and so had time to withdraw to higher terrain. Perhaps even that is looking at it from a human perspective. They probably just found themselves moving to higher terrain. Doing *this* because of *that* is the mind's way of cutting up reality; whereas nature lives in unconscious oneness with the whole. It is our purpose and destiny to bring a new dimension into this world by living in conscious oneness with the totality and conscious alignment with universal intelligence.

*Can the whole use the human mind to create things or bring about situations that are in alignment with its purpose?*

Yes, whenever there is inspiration, which translates as "in spirit," and enthusiasm, which means "in God," there is a creative empowerment that goes far beyond what a mere person is capable of.

## CHAPTER TEN

# A New Earth

Astronomers have discovered evidence to suggest that the universe came into existence fifteen billion years ago in a gigantic explosion and has been expanding ever since. Not only has it been expanding, but it is also growing in complexity and becoming more and more differentiated. Some scientists also postulate that this movement from unity to multiplicity will eventually become reversed. The universe will then stop expanding and begin to contract again and finally return to the unmanifested, the inconceivable no-thingness out of which it came—and perhaps repeat the cycles of birth, expansion, contraction, and death again and again. For what purpose? "Why does the universe go to all the bother of existing?" asks physicist Stephen Hawking, realizing at the same time that no mathematical model could ever supply the answer.

If you look within rather than only without, however, you discover that you have an inner and an outer purpose, and since you are a microcosmic reflection of the macrocosm, it follows that the universe too has an inner and outer purpose inseparable from yours. The outer purpose of the universe is to create form and experience the interaction of forms—the play, the dream, the drama, or whatever you choose to call it. Its inner purpose is to awaken to its formless essence. Then comes the reconciliation of outer and inner purpose: to bring that essence—consciousness—into the world of form and thereby transform the world. The ultimate purpose of that transformation goes far beyond anything the human mind can imagine or comprehend. And yet, on this planet at this time, that transformation is the task allotted us. That is the reconciliation of outer and inner purpose, the reconciliation of the world and God.

Before we look at what relevance the expansion and contraction of the universe has to your own life, we need to bear in mind here that nothing we say about the nature of the universe should be taken as an absolute truth. Neither concepts nor mathematical formulae can explain the infinite. No thought can encapsulate the vastness of the totality. Reality is a unified whole, but thought cuts it up into fragments. This gives rise to fundamental misperceptions, for example, that there are separate things and events, or that *this* is the cause of *that*. Every thought implies a perspective, and every perspective, by its very nature, implies limitation, which ultimately means that it is not true, at least not absolutely. Only the whole is true, but the whole cannot be spoken or thought. Seen from beyond the limitations of thinking and therefore incomprehensible to the human mind, everything is happening now. All that ever has been or will be is now, outside of time, which is a mental construct.

As an illustration of relative and absolute truth, consider the sunrise and sunset. When we say the sun rises in the morning and sets in the evening, that is true, but only relatively. In absolute terms, it is false. Only from the limited perspective of an observer on or near the planet's surface does the sun rise and set. If you were far out in space, you would see that the sun neither rises nor sets, but that it shines continuously. And yet, even after realizing that, we can continue to speak of the sunrise or sunset, still see its beauty, paint it, write poems about it, even though we now know that it is a relative rather than an absolute truth.

So let us continue to speak for a moment of another relative truth: the coming into form of the universe and its return to the formless, which implies the limited perspective of time, and see what relevance this has to your own life. The notion of "my own life" is, of course, another limited perspective created by thought, another relative truth. There is ultimately no such thing as "your" life, since you and life are not two, but one.

## A BRIEF HISTORY OF YOUR LIFE

The coming into manifestation of the world as well as its return to the unmanifested—its expansion and contraction— are two universal movements that we could call the out-going and the return home. Those two movements are reflected throughout the universe in many ways, such as in the incessant expansion and contraction of your heart, as well as in the inhalation and exhalation of your breath. They are also reflected in the cycles of sleep and wakeful-ness. Each night, without knowing it, you return to the unmanifested Source of all life when you enter the stage of deep, dreamless sleep, and then reemerge again in the morning, replenished.

Those two movements, the outgoing and the return, are also reflected in each person's life cycles. Out of nowhere, so to speak, "you" suddenly appear in this world. Birth is followed by expansion. There is not only physical growth, but also growth of knowledge, activities, possessions, expe-riences. Your sphere of influence expands and life becomes increasingly complex. This is a time when you are mainly concerned with finding or pursuing your outer purpose. Usually there is also a corresponding growth of the ego, which is identification with all the above things, and so your form identity becomes more and more defined. This is also the time when outer purpose—growth—tends to becomes usurped by the ego, which unlike nature does not know when to stop in its pursuit of expansion and has a voracious appetite for *more*.

And then, just when you thought you made it or that you belong here, the return movement begins. Perhaps people close to you begin to die, people who were a part of your world. Then your physical form weakens; your sphere of influence shrinks. Instead of becoming more, you now become less, and the ego reacts to this with increasing anxiety or depression. Your world is beginning to contract, and you may find you are not in control anymore. Instead of acting upon life, life now acts upon you by slowly reducing your world. The consciousness that identified with form is now experiencing the sunset, the dissolution of form. And then one day, you too disappear. Your armchair is still there. But instead of you sitting in it, there is just an empty space. You went back to where you came from just a few years ago.

Each person's life—each life-form, in fact—represents a world, a unique way in which the universe experiences itself. And when your form dissolves, a world comes to an end—one of countless worlds.

## AWAKENING AND
## THE RETURN MOVEMENT

The return movement in a person's life, the weakening or dissolution of form, whether through old age, illness, disability, loss, or some kind of personal tragedy, carries great potential for spiritual awakening—the dis-identification of consciousness from form. Since there is very little spiritual truth in our contemporary culture, not many people recognize this as an opportunity, and so when it happens to them or to someone close to them, they think there is something dreadfully wrong, something that should not be happening.

There is in our civilization a great deal of ignorance about the human condition, and the more spiritually ignorant you are, the more you suffer. For many people, particularly in the West, death is no more than an abstract concept, and so they have no idea what happens to the human form when it approaches dissolution. Most decrepit and old people are shut away in nursing homes. Dead bodies, which in some older cultures are on open display for all to see, are hidden away. Try to see a dead body, and you will find that it is virtually illegal, except if the deceased is a close family member. In funeral homes, they even apply makeup to the face. You are only allowed to see a sanitized version of death.

Since death is only an abstract concept to them, most

people are totally unprepared for the dissolution of form that awaits them. When it approaches, there is shock, incomprehension, despair, and great fear. Nothing makes sense anymore, because all the meaning and purpose that life had for them was associated with accumulating, succeeding, building, protecting, and sense gratification. It was associated with the outward movement and identification with form, that is to say, ego. Most people cannot conceive of any meaning when their life, their world, is being demolished. And yet, potentially, there is even deeper meaning here than in the outward movement.

It is precisely through the onset of old age, through loss or personal tragedy, that the spiritual dimension would traditionally come into people's lives. This is to say, their inner purpose would emerge only as their outer purpose collapsed and the shell of the ego would begin to crack open. Such events represent the beginning of the return movement toward the dissolution of form. In most ancient cultures, there must have been an intuitive understanding of this process, which is why old people were respected and revered. They were the repositories of wisdom and provided the dimension of depth without which no civilization can survive for long. In our civilization, which is totally identified with the outer and ignorant of the inner dimension of spirit, the word *old* has mainly negative connotations. It equals useless and so we regard it as almost an insult to refer to someone as old. To avoid the word, we use euphemisms such as elderly and senior. The First Nation's "grandmother" is a figure of great dignity. Today's "granny" is at best cute. Why is old considered useless? Because in old age, the emphasis shifts from doing to Being, and our civilization, which is lost in doing, knows nothing of Being. It asks: Being? What do you do with it?

In some people, the outward movement of growth and expansion gets severely disrupted by a seemingly premature onset of the return movement, the dissolving of form. In some cases, it is a temporary disruption; in others a permanent one. We believe that a young child should not have to face death, but the fact is that some children do have to face the death of one or both parents through illness or accident—or even the possibility of their own death. Some children are born with disabilities that severely restrict the natural expansion of their lives. Or some severe limitation comes into a person's life at a relatively young age.

The disruption of the outward movement at a time when it is "not meant to be happening" can also potentially bring forth an early spiritual awakening in a person. Ultimately, nothing happens that is not meant to happen, which is to say, nothing happens that is not part of the greater whole and its purpose. Thus, destruction or disruption of outer purpose can lead to finding your inner purpose and subsequently the arising of a deeper outer purpose that is aligned with the inner. Children who have suffered greatly often grow into young adults who are mature beyond their years.

What is lost on the level of form is gained on the level of essence. In the traditional figure of the "blind seer" or the "wounded healer" of ancient cultures and legend, some great loss or disability on the level of form has become an opening into spirit. When you have had a direct experience of the unstable nature of all forms, you will likely never overvalue form again and thus lose yourself by blindly pursuing it or attaching yourself to it.

The opportunity that the dissolution of form, and in particular, old age, represents is only just beginning to be recognized in our contemporary culture. In the majority of people, that opportunity is still tragically missed, because the ego identifies with the return movement just as it identified with the outward movement. This results in a hardening of the egoic shell, a contraction rather than an opening. The diminished ego then spends the rest of its days whining or complaining, trapped in fear or anger, self-pity, guilt, blame, or other negative mental-emotional states or avoidance strategies, such as attachment to memories and thinking and talking about the past.

When the ego is no longer identified with the return movement in a person's life, old age or approaching death becomes what it is meant to be: an opening into the realm of spirit. I have met old people who were living embodiments of this process. They had become radiant. Their weakening forms had become transparent to the light of consciousness.

On the new earth, old age will be universally recognized and highly valued as a time for the flowering of consciousness. For those who are still lost in the outer circumstances of their lives, it will be a time of a late homecoming, when they awaken to their inner purpose. For many others, it will represent an intensification and a culmination of the awakening process.

## AWAKENING AND
## THE OUTGOING MOVEMENT

The natural expansion of one's life that comes with the outward movement has traditionally been usurped by the ego and used for its own expansion. "Look what *I* can do. I bet *you* can't do that," says the small child to another as he discovers the increasing strength and abilities of his body. That is one of the ego's first attempts to enhance itself through identification with the outward movement and the concept of "more than you" and to strengthen itself by diminishing others. It is, of course, only the beginning of the ego's many misperceptions.

However, as your awareness increases and the ego is no longer running your life, you don't have to wait for your world to shrink or collapse through old age or personal tragedy in order for you to awaken to your inner purpose.

As the new consciousness is beginning to emerge on the planet, an increasing number of people no longer need to be shaken to have an awakening. They embrace the awakening process voluntarily even while still engaged in the outward cycle of growth and expansion. When that cycle is no longer usurped by the ego, the spiritual dimension will come into this world through the outward movement—thought, speech, action, creation—as powerfully as through the return movement—stillness, Being, and dissolution of form.

Until now, human intelligence, which is no more than a minute aspect of universal intelligence, has been distorted and misused by the ego. I call that "intelligence in the service of madness." Splitting the atom requires great intelligence. Using that intelligence for building and stockpiling atom bombs is insane or at best extremely unintelligent. Stupidity is relatively harmless, but intelligent stupidity is highly dangerous. This intelligent stupidity, for which one could find countless obvious examples, is threatening our survival as a species.

Without the impairment of egoic dysfunction, our intelligence comes into full alignment with the outgoing cycle of universal intelligence and its impulse to create. We become conscious participants in the creation of form. It is not we who create, but universal intelligence that creates through us. We don't identify with what we create and so don't lose ourselves in what we do. We are learning that the act of creation may involve energy of the highest intensity, but that is not "hard work" or stressful. We need to understand the difference between stress and intensity, as we shall see. Struggle or stress is a sign that the ego has returned, as are negative reactions when we encounter obstacles.

The force behind the ego's wanting creates "enemies," that is to say, reaction in the form of an opposing force equal in intensity. The stronger the ego, the stronger the sense of separateness between people. The only actions that do not cause opposing reactions are those that are aimed at the good of all. They are inclusive, not exclusive. They join; they don't separate. They are not for "my" country but for all of humanity, not for "my" religion but the emergence of consciousness in all human beings, not for "my" species but for all sentient beings and all of nature.

We are also learning that action, although necessary, is only a secondary factor in manifesting our external reality. The primary factor in creation is consciousness. No matter how active we are, how much effort we make, our state of consciousness creates our world, and if there is no change on that inner level, no amount of action will make any difference. We would only re-create modified versions of the same world again and again, a world that is an external reflection of the ego.

## CONSCIOUSNESS

Consciousness is already conscious. It is the unmanifested, the eternal. The universe, however, is only gradually becoming conscious. Consciousness itself is timeless and therefore does not evolve. It was never born and does not die. When consciousness becomes the manifested universe, it appears to be subject to time and to undergo an evolutionary process. No human mind is capable of comprehending fully the reason for this process. But we can glimpse it within ourselves and become a conscious participant in it.

Consciousness is the intelligence, the organizing principle behind the arising of form. Consciousness has been preparing forms for millions of years so that it can express itself through them in the manifested.

Although the unmanifested realm of pure consciousness could be considered another dimension, it is not separate from this dimension of form. Form and formlessness interpenetrate. The unmanifested flows into this dimension as awareness, inner space, Presence. How does it do that? Through the human form that becomes conscious and thus fulfills its destiny. The human form was created for this higher purpose, and millions of other forms prepared the ground for it.

Consciousness incarnates into the manifested dimension, that is to say, it becomes form. When it does so, it enters a dreamlike state. Intelligence remains, but consciousness becomes unconscious of itself. It loses itself in form, becomes identified with forms. This could be described as the descent of the divine into matter. At that stage in the evolution of the universe, the entire outgoing movement takes place in that dreamlike state. Glimpses of awakening come only at the moment of the dissolution of an individual form, that is to say, death. And then begins the next incarnation, the next identification with form, the next individual dream that is part of the collective dream. When the lion tears apart the body of the zebra, the consciousness that incarnated into the zebra-form detaches itself from the dissolving form and for a brief moment awakens to its essential immortal nature as consciousness; and then immediately falls back into sleep and reincarnates into another form. When the lion becomes old and cannot hunt anymore, as it draws its last breath, there is again the briefest of glimpses of an awakening, followed by another dream of form.

On our planet, the human ego represents the final stage of universal sleep, the identification of consciousness with form. It was a necessary stage in the evolution of consciousness.

The human brain is a highly differentiated form through which consciousness enters this dimension. It contains approximately one hundred billion nerve cells (called neurons), about the same number as there are stars in our galaxy, which could be seen as a macrocosmic brain. The brain does not create consciousness, but consciousness created the brain, the most complex physical form on earth, for its expression. When the brain gets damaged, it does not mean you lose consciousness. It means consciousness can no longer use that form to enter this dimension. You cannot lose consciousness because it is, in essence, who you are. You can only lose something that you have, but you cannot lose something that you are.

## AWAKENED DOING

Awakened doing is the outer aspect of the next stage in the evolution of consciousness on our planet. The closer we get to the end of our present evolutionary stage, the more dysfunctional the ego becomes, in the same way that a caterpillar becomes dysfunctional just before it transforms into a butterfly. But the new consciousness is arising even as the old dissolves.

We are in the midst of a momentous event in the evolution of human consciousness, but they won't be talking about it in the news tonight. On our planet, and perhaps simultaneously in many parts of our galaxy and beyond, consciousness is awakening from the dream of form. This does not mean all forms (the world) are going to dissolve, although quite a few almost certainly will. It means consciousness can now begin to create form without losing itself in it. It can remain conscious of itself, even while it creates and experiences form. Why should it continue to create and experience form? For the enjoyment of it. How does consciousness do that? Through awakened humans who have learned the meaning of *awakened doing.*

Awakened doing is the alignment of your outer purpose— what you do—with your inner purpose—awakening and staying awake. Through awakened doing, you become one with the outgoing purpose of the universe. Consciousness flows through you into this world. It flows into your thoughts and inspires them. It flows into what you do and guides and empowers it.

Not *what* you do, but *how* you do what you do determines whether you are fulfilling your destiny. And how you do what you do is determined by your state of consciousness.

A reversal of your priorities comes about when the main purpose for doing what you do becomes the doing itself, or rather, the current of consciousness that flows into what you do. That current of consciousness is what determines quality. Another way of putting it: In any situation and in whatever you do, your state of consciousness is the primary factor; the situation and what you do is secondary. "Future" success is dependent upon and inseparable from the consciousness out of which the actions emanate. That can be either the reactive force of the ego or the alert attention of awakened consciousness. All truly successful action comes out of that field of alert attention, rather than from ego and conditioned, unconscious thinking.

## THE THREE MODALITIES
## OF AWAKENED DOING

There are three ways in which consciousness can flow into what you do and thus through you into this world, three modalities in which you can align your life with the creative power of the universe. Modality means the underlying energy-frequency that flows into what you do and connects your actions with the awakened consciousness that is emerging into this world. What you do will be dysfunctional and of the ego unless it arises out of one of these three modalities. They may change during the course of a day, although one of them may be dominant during a certain stage in your life. Each modality is appropriate to certain situations.

The modalities of awakened doing are acceptance, enjoyment, and enthusiasm. Each one represents a certain vibrational frequency of consciousness. You need to be vigilant to make sure that one of them operates whenever you are engaged in doing anything at all—from the most simple task to the most complex. If you are not in the state of either acceptance, enjoyment, or enthusiasm, look closely and you will find that you are creating suffering for yourself and others.

## ACCEPTANCE

Whatever you cannot enjoy doing, you can at least accept that this is what you have to do. Acceptance means: For now, this is what this situation, this moment, requires me to do, and so I do it willingly. We already spoke at length about the importance of inner acceptance of what *happens*, and acceptance of what you have to *do* is just another aspect of it. For example, you probably won't be able to enjoy changing the flat tire on your car at night in the middle of nowhere and in pouring rain, let alone be enthusiastic about it, but you can bring acceptance to it. Performing an action in the state of acceptance means you are at peace while you do it. That peace is a subtle energy vibration which then flows into what you do. On the surface, acceptance looks like a passive state, but in reality it is active and creative because it brings something entirely new into this world. That peace, that subtle energy vibration, is consciousness, and one of the ways in which it enters this world is through surrendered action, one aspect of which is acceptance.

If you can neither enjoy or bring acceptance to what you do—stop. Otherwise, you are not taking responsibility for the only thing you can really take responsibility for, which also happens to be one thing that really matters: your state of consciousness. And if you are not taking responsibility for your state of consciousness, you are not taking re-sponsibility for life.

## ENJOYMENT

The peace that comes with surrendered action turns to a sense of aliveness when you actually enjoy what you are doing. Enjoyment is the second modality of awakened do-ing. On the new earth, enjoyment will replace wanting as the motivating power behind people's actions. Wanting arises from the ego's delusion that you are a separate frag-ment that is disconnected from the power that lies behind all creation. Through enjoyment, you link into that univer-sal creative power itself.

When you make the present moment, instead of past and future, the focal point of your life, your ability to enjoy what you do—and with it the quality of your life—increases dramatically. Joy is the dynamic aspect of Being. When the creative power of the universe becomes con-scious of itself, it manifests as joy. You don't have to wait for something "meaningful" to come into your life so that you can finally enjoy what you do. There is more meaning in joy than you will ever need. The "waiting to start living" syndrome is one of the most common delusions of the un-conscious state. Expansion and positive change on the outer level is much more likely to come into your life if you can enjoy what you are doing already, instead of waiting for some change so that you can start enjoying what you do. Don't ask your mind for permission to enjoy what you do. All you will get is plenty of reasons why you can't enjoy it. "Not now," the mind will say. "Can't you see I'm busy? There's no time. Maybe tomorrow you can start enjoy-ing . . . ." That tomorrow will never come unless you begin enjoying what you are doing now.

When you say, I enjoy doing this or that, it is really a misperception. It makes it appear that the joy comes from what you do, but that is not the case. Joy does not come from what you do, it flows into what you do and thus into this world from deep within you. The misperception that joy comes from what you do is normal, and it is also dan-gerous, because it creates the belief that joy is something that can be derived from something else, such as an activity or thing. You then look to the world to bring you joy, hap-piness. But it cannot do that. This is why many people live in constant frustration. The world is not giving them what they think they need.

Then what is the relationship between something that you do and the state of joy? You will enjoy any activity in which you are fully present, any activity that is not just a means to an end. It isn't the action you perform that you really enjoy, but the deep sense of aliveness that flows into it. That aliveness is one with who you are. This means that when you enjoy doing something, you are really experiencing the joy of Being in its dynamic aspect. That's why anything you enjoy doing connects you with the power behind all creation.

Here is a spiritual practice that will bring empowerment and creative expansion into your life. Make a list of a number of everyday routine activities that you perform frequently. Include activities that you may consider uninteresting, boring, tedious, irritating, or stressful. But don't include anything that you hate or detest doing. That's a case either for acceptance or for stopping what you do. The list may include traveling to and from work, buying groceries, doing your laundry, or anything that you find tedious or stressful in your daily work. Then, whenever you are engaged in those activities, let them be a vehicle for alertness. Be absolutely present in what you do and sense the alert, alive stillness within you in the background of the activity. You will soon find that what you do in such a state of heightened awareness, instead of being stressful, tedious, or irritating, is actually becoming enjoyable. To be more precise, what you are enjoying is not really the outward action but the inner dimension of consciousness that flows into the action. This is finding the joy of Being in what you are doing. If you feel your life lacks significance or is too stressful or tedious, it is because you haven't brought that dimension into your life yet. Being conscious in what you do has not yet become your main aim.

The new earth arises as more and more people discover

that their main purpose in life is to bring the light of consciousness into this world and so use whatever they do as a vehicle for consciousness.

The joy of Being is the joy of being conscious.

Awakened consciousness then takes over from ego and begins to run your life. You may then find that an activity that you have been engaged in for a long time naturally begins to expand into something much bigger when it becomes empowered by consciousness.

Some of those people who, through creative action, enrich the lives of many others simply do what they enjoy doing most without wanting to achieve or become anything through that activity. They may be musicians, artists, writers, scientists, teachers, or builders, or they may bring into manifestation new social or business structures (enlightened businesses). Sometimes for a few years their sphere of influence remains small; and then it can happen that suddenly or gradually a wave of creative empowerment flows into what they do, and their activity expands beyond anything they could have imagined and touches countless others. In addition to enjoyment, an intensity is now added to what they do and with it comes a creativity that goes beyond anything an ordinary human could accomplish.

But don't let it go to your head, because up there is where a remnant of ego may be hiding. You are still an ordinary human. What is extraordinary is what comes through you into this world. But that essence you share with all beings. The fourteenth-century Persian poet and Sufi master Hafiz expresses this truth beautifully: "I am a hole in a flute that the Christ's breath moves through. Listen to this music."[1]

## ENTHUSIASM

Then there is another way of creative manifestation that may come to those who remain true to their inner purpose of awakening. Suddenly one day they know what their outer purpose is. They have a great vision, a goal, and from then on they work toward implementing that goal. Their goal or vision is usually connected in some way to something that on a smaller scale they are doing and enjoy doing already. This is where the third modality of awakened doing arises: enthusiasm.

Enthusiasm means there is deep enjoyment in what you do plus the added element of a goal or a vision that you work toward. When you add a goal to the enjoyment of what you do, the energy-field or vibrational frequency changes. A certain degree of what we might call structural tension is now added to enjoyment, and so it turns into enthusiasm. At the height of creative activity fueled by enthusiasm, there will be enormous intensity and energy behind what you do. You will feel like an arrow that is moving toward the target—and enjoying the journey.

To an onlooker, it may appear that you are under stress,

but the intensity of enthusiasm has nothing to do with stress. When you want to arrive at your goal more than you want to be doing what you are doing, you become stressed. The balance between enjoyment and structural tension is lost, and the latter has won. When there is stress, it is usually a sign that the ego has returned, and you are cutting yourself off from the creative power of the universe. Instead, there is only the force and strain of egoic wanting, and so you have to struggle and "work hard" to make it. Stress always diminishes both the quality and effectiveness of what you do under its influence. There is also a strong link between stress and negative emotions, such as anxiety and anger. It is toxic to the body and is now becoming recognized as one of the main causes of the so-called degenerative diseases such as cancer and heart disease.

Unlike stress, enthusiasm has a high energy frequency and so resonates with the creative power of the universe. This is why Ralph Waldo Emerson said that, "Nothing great has ever been achieved without enthusiasm."[2] The word *enthusiasm* comes from ancient Greek—*en* and *theos*, meaning God. And the related word *enthousiazein* means "to be possessed by a god." With enthusiasm you will find that you don't have to do it all by yourself. In fact, there is nothing of significance that you *can* do by yourself. Sustained enthusiasm brings into existence a wave of creative energy, and all you have to do then is "ride the wave."

Enthusiasm brings an enormous empowerment into what you do, so that all those who have not accessed that power would look upon "your" achievements in awe and may equate them with who you are. You, however, know the truth that Jesus pointed to when he said, "I can of my own self do nothing."[3] Unlike egoic wanting, which creates opposition in direct proportion to the intensity of its wanting, enthusiasm never opposes. It is non-confrontational. Its activity does not create winners and losers. It is based on inclusion, not exclusion, of others. It does not need to use and manipulate people, because it is the power of creation itself and so does not need to take energy from some secondary source. The ego's wanting always tries to take from something or someone; enthusiasm gives out of its own abundance. When enthusiasm encounters obstacles in the form of adverse situations or uncooperative people, it never attacks but walks around them or by yielding or embracing turns the opposing energy into a helpful one, the foe into a friend.

Enthusiasm and the ego cannot coexist. One implies the absence of the other. Enthusiasm knows where it is going, but at the same time, it is deeply at one with the present moment, the source of its aliveness, its joy, and its power. Enthusiasm "wants" nothing because it lacks nothing. It is at one with life and no matter how dynamic the enthusiasm-inspired activities are, you don't lose yourself in them. And there remains always a still but intensely alive space at the center of the wheel, a core of peace in the midst of activity that is both the source of all and untouched by it all.

Through enthusiasm you enter into full alignment with the outgoing creative principle of the universe, but without identifying with its creations, that is to say, without ego. Where there is no identification, there is no attachment— one of the great sources of suffering. Once a wave of creative energy has passed, structural tension diminishes again and joy in what you are doing remains. Nobody can live in enthusiasm all the time. A new wave of creative energy may come later and lead to renewed enthusiasm.

When the return movement toward the dissolution of form sets in, enthusiasm no longer serves you. Enthusiasm belongs to the outgoing cycle of life. It is only through surrender that you can align yourself with the return movement—the journey home.

To sum up: Enjoyment of what you are doing, combined with a goal or vision that you work toward, becomes enthusiasm. Even though you have a goal, what you are doing in the present moment needs to remain the focal point of your attention; otherwise, you will fall out of alignment with universal purpose. Make sure your vision or goal is not an inflated image of yourself and therefore a concealed form of ego, such as wanting to become a movie star, a famous writer, or a wealthy entrepreneur. Also make sure your goal is not focused on *having* this or that, such as a mansion by the sea, your own company, or ten million dollars in the bank. An enlarged image of yourself or a vision of yourself *having* this or that are all static goals and therefore don't empower you. Instead, make sure your goals are dynamic, that is to say, point toward an *activity* that you are engaged in and through which you are connected to other human beings as well as to the whole. Instead of seeing yourself as a famous actor and writer and so on, see yourself inspiring countless people with your work and enriching their lives. Feel how that activity enriches or deepens not only your life but that of countless others. Feel yourself being an opening through which energy flows from the unmanifested Source of all life through you for the benefit of all.

All this implies that your goal or vision is then already a reality within you, on the level of mind and of feeling. Enthusiasm is the power that transfers the mental blueprint into the physical dimension. That is the creative use of mind, and that is why there is no wanting involved. You cannot manifest what you want; you can only manifest what you already have. You may get what you want through hard work and stress, but that is not the way of the new earth. Jesus gave the key to the creative use of mind and to the conscious manifestation of form when he said, "Whatever you ask in prayer, believe that you have received it, and it will be yours."[4]

## THE FREQUENCY-HOLDERS

The outward movement into form does not express itself with equal intensity in all people. Some feel a strong urge to build, create, become involved, achieve, make an impact upon the world. If they are unconscious, their ego will, of course, take over and use the energy of the outgoing cycle for its own purposes. This, however, also greatly reduces the flow of creative energy available to them and increasingly they need to rely on "efforting" to get what they want. If they are conscious, those people in whom the outward movement is strong will be highly creative. Others, after the natural expansion that comes with growing up has run its course, lead an outwardly unremarkable, seemingly more passive and relatively uneventful existence.

They are more inward looking by nature, and for them the outward movement into form is minimal. They would rather return home than go out. They have no desire to get strongly involved in or change the world. If they have any ambitions, they usually don't go beyond finding something to do that gives them a degree of independence. Some of them find it hard to fit into this world. Some are lucky enough to find a protective niche where they can lead a relatively sheltered life, a job that provides them with a regular income or a small business of their own. Some may feel drawn toward living in a spiritual community or monastery. Others may become dropouts and live on the margins of a society they feel they have little in common with. Some turn to drugs because they find living in this world too painful. Others eventually become healers or spiritual teachers, that is to say, teachers of Being.

In past ages, they would probably have been called contemplatives. There is no place for them, it seems, in our contemporary civilization. On the arising new earth, however, their role is just as vital as that of the creators, the doers, the reformers. Their function is to anchor the frequency of the new consciousness on this planet. I call them the frequency-holders. They are here to generate consciousness through the activities of daily life, through their interactions with others as well as through "just being."

In this way, they endow the seemingly insignificant with profound meaning. Their task is to bring spacious stillness into this world by being absolutely present in whatever they do. There is consciousness and therefore quality in what they do, even the simplest task. Their purpose is to do everything in a sacred manner. As each human being is an integral part of the collective human consciousness, they affect the world much more deeply than is visible on the surface of their lives.

## THE NEW EARTH IS NO UTOPIA

Is the notion of a new earth not just another utopian vision? Not at all. All utopian visions have this in common:

the mental projection of a future time when all will be well, we will be saved, there will be peace and harmony and the end of our problems. There have been many such utopian visions. Some ended in disappointment, others in disaster.

At the core of all utopian visions lies one of the main structural dysfunctions of the old consciousness: looking to the future for salvation. The only existence the future actually has is as a thought form in your mind, so when you look to the future for salvation, you are unconsciously looking to your own mind for salvation. You are trapped in form, and that is ego.

"And I saw a new heaven and a new earth,"[5] writes the biblical prophet. The foundation for a new earth is a new heaven—the awakened consciousness. The earth—external reality—is only its outer reflection. The arising of a new heaven and by implication a new earth are not future events that are going to make us free. Nothing is *going to* make us free because only the present moment can make us free. That realization is the awakening. Awakening as a future event has no meaning because awakening is the realization of Presence. So the new heaven, the awakened consciousness, is not a future state to be achieved. A new heaven and a new earth are arising within you at this moment, and if they are not arising at this moment, they are no more than a thought in your head and therefore not arising at all.

What did Jesus tell his disciples? "Heaven is right here in the midst of you."[6]

In the Sermon on the Mount, Jesus makes a prediction that to this day few people have understood. He says, "Blessed are the meek, for they shall inherit the earth."[7] In modern versions of the Bible, "meek" is translated as humble. Who are the meek or the humble, and what does it mean that they shall inherit the earth?

The meek are the egoless. They are those who have awakened to their essential true nature as consciousness and recognize that essence in all "others," all life-forms. They live in the surrendered state and so feel their oneness with the whole and the Source. They embody the awakened consciousness that is changing all aspects of life on our planet, including nature, because life on earth is inseparable from the human consciousness that perceives and interacts with it. That is the sense in which the meek will inherit the earth.

A new species is arising on the planet. It is arising now, and you are it!

# NOTES

## CHAPTER ONE

1 Revelation 21:1 and Isaiah 65:17 (New Revised Standard Version)

## CHAPTER TWO

1 Matthew 5:3 (New Revised Standard Version)
2 Philippians 4:7 (New Revised Standard Version)

## CHAPTER THREE

1 Luke 6:41 (New Revised Standard Version)
2 John 14:6 (New Revised Standard Version)
3 Halevi, Yossie K., "Introspective as a Prerequisite for Peace," *New York Times*, September 7, 2002
4 U.S. Department of Justice, Bureau of Justice Statistics, Prison Statistics, June, 2004
5 Einstein, Albert, *Mein Weltbild,* 25th Edition (Frankfurt: Ullstein Verlag, 1993), 42. Translation by Eckhart Tolle

## CHAPTER FOUR

1 Shakespeare, William, *Macbeth*. Signet Classic Edition (New York: New American Library). Edited by Sylvan Barnet

2 Shakespeare, William, *Hamlet*. Signet Classic Edition (New York: New American Library). Edited by Sylvan Barnet

CHAPTER SIX

1  Matthew 5:48 (New Revised Standard Version)

CHAPTER SEVEN

1 Luke 6:38 (New Revised Standard Version)

2 Mark 4:25 (New Revised Standard Version)

3 I Corinthians 3:19 (New Revised Standard Version)

4 Tzu, Lao, *Tao Te Ching,* chapter 28

5 Ibid, chapter 22

6 Luke 14:10-11 (New Revised Standard Version)

7 *Kena Upanishad*

CHAPTER EIGHT

1 Ecclesiasties 1:8 (New Revised Standard Version)

2 *A Course in Miracles*, Workbook, Part I, Lesson 5 (California: Foundation for Inner Peace, Glen Allen, 1990), 8.

3 Luke 17: 20-21 (New Revised Standard Version)

4 Nietzsche, Friedriche, *Thus Spake Zarathustra: A Book for All and None* (New York: Viking, 1954), 288

5 Genesis 2:7 (New Revised Standard Version)

CHAPTER NINE

1 John 5:30 and John 14:10 (New Revised Standard Version)

2 Matthew 6:28-29 (New Revised Standard Version)

CHAPTER TEN

1 Hafiz, *The Gift* (New York: Penguin, Arkana, 1999). Translated by Daniel Ladinsky

2 Emerson, Ralph Waldo, "Circles" in *Ralph Waldo Emerson: Selected Essays, Lectures, and Poems* (New York: Bantam Classics).

3 John 5:30 (New Revised Standard Version)

4 Mark 11:24 (New Revised Standard Version)

5 Revelation 21:1 (New Revised Standard Version)

6 Luke 17:21 (New Revised Standard Version)

7 Matthew 5:5 (New Revised Standard Version)